The Future of Childhood

In this ground-breaking text, Alan Prout discusses the place of children and childhood in contemporary society. He critically examines 'the new social studies of childhood', reconsidering some of their key assumptions and positions, and arguing that childhood is heterogeneous and complex. The study of childhood requires a broad set of intellectual resources and an interdisciplinary approach.

Chapters include discussion of:

- The changing character of contemporary childhood, and the shifting boundary between adulthood and childhood.
- The emergence of childhood studies in the nineteenth and twentieth centuries.
- The nature/culture dichotomy.
- The role of material artefacts and technologies in the construction of contemporary childhood.

This book is essential reading for students and academics in the field of childhood studies, sociology and education.

Alan Prout is Professor of Sociology and was formerly Director of the ESRC Children 5–16 Programme, University of Stirling.

The Future of Childhood series
Series Editor: Alan Prout

The Future of Childhood

Towards the interdisciplinary study of children

Alan Prout

RoutledgeFalmer
Taylor & Francis Group

LONDON AND NEW YORK

First published 2005
by RoutledgeFalmer
2 Park Square, Milton Park, Abingdon, Oxon OX14 4RN

Simultaneously published in the USA and Canada
by RoutledgeFalmer
270 Madison Ave, New York, NY 10016

RoutledgeFalmer is an imprint of the Taylor & Francis Group

© 2005 Alan Prout

Typeset in Bembo by
Florence Production Ltd, Stoodleigh, Devon
Printed and bound in Great Britain by
TJ International Ltd, Padstow, Cornwall

British Library Cataloguing in Publication Data
A catalogue record for this book is available from the British Library

Library of Congress Cataloguing in Publication Data
Prout, Alan.
    The future of childhood / Alan Prout.
        p. cm. – (The future of childhood series)
    Includes bibliographical references and index.
    1. Children – Social conditions – 20th century.   2. Children –
Social conditions – 21st century.   3. Children – Study and teaching.
I. Title.   II. Series.
HQ767.9.P76 2004
305.23'09'04 – dc22 2004003839

ISBN 0–415–25674–7 (hbk)
ISBN 0–415–25675–5 (pbk)

This book is dedicated to
my parents, Mary and Eric

Contents

Acknowledgements

I am grateful to many colleagues in the childhood studies field for their contributions to our debates and discussions over many years. I am also indebted to Hannah Buchanan-Smith, a primatologist at Stirling University, for introducing me to contemporary thinking in evolutionary biology. I thank all those involved in the discussion of earlier versions of Chapter 3: members of the Childhood Section of the German Sociological Association at their annual meeting in Berlin during June 2002; colleagues at the Centre for Lifelong Learning, Roskilde University, Denmark (where I was Visiting Professor in Spring 2002); and participants at a conference held at the University of Wupertaal, Germany, in May 2003. Finally, I give my special thanks to Pia for her unfailing support, intellectual encouragement and patience before, during and after the writing of this book, large parts of which were written in Copenhagen.

Acknowledgements

Introduction

This book grew out of my involvement with what have come to be known as the 'new social studies of childhood'. During the 1980s social scientists around the world began to express their growing dissatisfaction with the way in which their disciplines dealt with childhood. Among some, especially those in psychology, which has a substantial history of studying childhood, this took the form of a critique centred on the notion of 'development'. While not rejected, this concept was increasingly criticized for its lack of attention to the social and historical context of childhood and the highly variable circumstances in which children grow up. This attention to context led to certain aspects of conventional approaches being criticized. These included the assumption that childhood can be treated as a universal, biologically given phenomenon as well as the determinedly individual focus of mainstream child development studies. Both the form of childhood as a social and cultural institution and the process of 'growing up' became seen as dependent on their context rather than naturally unfolding processes.

Many of the sociologists and anthropologists who had also become interested in childhood shared these critical themes. Their disciplines were, of course, already primed to recognize the importance of social and cultural context. In their case, however, there was an additional concern about the general neglect of children and childhood in sociology and anthropology, an unease that was linked to dissatisfaction with the inadequacy of the concepts that dominated the (relatively little) sociological and anthropological thinking that had been done. Here too there was antipathy towards decontextualized ideas of development but in these disciplines the critique was focused on the concept of socialization. It was argued that this was too often treated as a one-way effect of (adult) society on individual children. This not only led to a neglect of children, because they were seen as not-yet-social beings, but was also inattentive to children's active social participation, their agency in social life and their collective life. Such critiques led to an upsurge of research activity in which childhood was examined as a social construction and children studied not as passive objects of socialization but as social actors in their own right. Because this effort had a multi- and interdisciplinary dimension from the start, attracting the contributions of, among others, sociologists, anthropologists, historians, psychologists and geographers, it adopted a cross-disciplinary name, 'the new social studies of childhood', although much of their dynamic actually came from sociology.

The scholarly writing and research that this movement has produced over the last two decades is impressive. This book builds on this work and is a contribution to its continuation. However, it makes this contribution not by simply endorsing the record so far but by critically reconsidering some of its assumptions and positions. In essence it argues that, productive though the new social studies of childhood have been, the intellectual limits of the programme are increasingly apparent. At the core of this argument is a conviction that childhood is not best studied within a framework built from and/or implicitly assuming a set of oppositional dichotomies. This, I argue, characterizes many of the new social studies of childhood. In fact their founding idea expresses just such an opposition because childhood is treated as a social construction. This social view of childhood is counter-posed to a natural or biological one. From this point of view the new social studies are a reverse discourse standing in an oppositional relationship to older, biologically centred ideas of childhood. This is understandable because, in order to establish their distinct contribution, novel intellectual initiatives, such as the new social studies of childhood, frequently overstate their case, overplaying their difference from earlier formulations. Such a strategy is even excusable if it gives rise to new research questions and findings, as is certainly the case for the new social studies.

However, I believe that the phase in which the new social studies of childhood needed to emphasize their differences with other approaches is coming to an end. There is, for example, a tendency to repeat the basic ideas, such as 'children are social actors', as if these were still novel insights that have not already won wide agreement. In order to move the field on it is necessary to reconnect the social study of childhood with those aspects of earlier or different approaches that have something valuable to offer. The fundamental reason for this is that, however illuminating it is to regard childhood as a social phenomenon, it is not and never has been purely social. In fact it is hard to envisage what a 'purely social' phenomenon would look like. Social relations are already heterogeneous, that is they are made up from a wide variety of material, discursive, cultural, natural, technological, human and non-human resources. Childhood, then, like all phenomena, is heterogeneous, complex and emergent, and, because this is so, its understanding requires a broad set of intellectual resources, an inter-disciplinary approach and an open-minded process of enquiry.

This is the general argument that I set out to make in this book. The argument is unfolded over five chapters. Chapter 1 examines the changing social and cultural character of contemporary childhood. It is suggested that, as part of a complex and contradictory process of social, economic, cultural and technological change, the boundary between adulthood and childhood that was established in the modern period is weakening. The diversity of forms that childhood can take is expanding, or at least becoming more visible. As a consequence, there is a growing appreciation of the need to revize the assumption that childhood is a unitary phenomenon. The idea that children are social actors, which is not confined to academic thinking, is emerging as part of this general change, as well as feeding back into it. In the face of the changing character of contemporary childhood, new ways of representing, seeing and understanding children and childhood are needed.

Chapter 2 looks back from the contemporary scene, surveying the emergence of the study of childhood in the nineteenth and twentieth centuries. This reveals a tendency towards separating the social and cultural aspects of childhood from the biological ones. The problems that this creates are usually dealt with in one of two ways. The first is reductionist: the attempt to explain all aspects of childhood in terms of a single principle, be this biological or social. The second is additive: nature and culture remain as separate, incommensurable entities that are then seen as contributing a distinct proportion of the material that goes into the making of childhood. The discussion is consequently about the proportion of each that goes into the mixture. Both the reductionist and the additive approach encourage the study of childhood to proceed on separate social and biological tracks. This poses the problem of finding a framework within which childhood can be seen as simultaneously part of culture and nature while not treating either as a distinct, autonomous or pure entity.

Chapter 3 takes up this theme but focuses specifically on the new social studies of childhood, suggesting that their analytical approach has also been marked by a broader set of mutually exclusive oppositions. These include culture and nature but also familiar sociological oppositions, such as 'being' and 'becoming', 'structure' and 'agency' and so on. Strategies for moving beyond such dualistic oppositions are explored in a discussion that draws on innovative ideas coming from actor–network theory and complexity theory. These are related to current discussion in childhood studies about generational relations and the life course perspective.

Chapter 4 further examines the requirement that childhood studies move beyond the opposition of nature and culture. Social scientists have bracketed out biology in their accounts of childhood and the chapter retraces the steps through which this came about. It is argued that the cultural/social and the biological are not 'pure entities' but are, rather, mutually implicated with each other at every level. The natural sciences through which biological entities and processes are apprehended both shape and are shaped by culture. The human species evolved through a complex process that includes both genes and culture. Crucially humans have evolved both language and technology to a higher level than other species, resulting in a hybrid form that cannot be reduced to either biology or culture.

A characteristic of the species is its very extended juvenile stage, part of an evolutionary strategy that requires the transmission of culture and the acquisition of skills. The human being is therefore both biologically and socially unfinished. Furthermore, like adults, children's capacities are extended and supplemented by all kinds of material artefacts and technologies, which are also hybrids of nature and culture. This shapes the constitution of childhood and the experiences and actions of children.

Chapter 5 concludes the argument by examining the crucial role played by material artefacts and technologies in the construction of contemporary childhood. Childhood is to be regarded as a collection of diverse, emergent assemblages constructed from heterogeneous materials. These materials are biological, social, cultural, technological and so on. However, they are not seen as pure materials but are themselves hybrids produced through time. Three such assemblages are used to illustrate this idea and to speculate on trends in the construction of contemporary childhood. These cluster around the relationships between childhood and information and communication technologies; genetics; and psychopharmaceuticals.

The problems addressed in this book are not unique to childhood studies. The desire to find more flexible, non-dualistic ways of thinking, which can express the ambiguity of contemporary life, is widely found across many disciplines and in relation to many different empirical topics. Although dualistic oppositions are to be found within many systems of thought, their use became particularly intense and prominent in the modern period. However, as modernity reaches the limit of its possibilities, and as the paradoxes and problems that this produces become more apparent, so, too, modernist patterns of thought have become more problematic and subject to critical scrutiny. Indeed the present period is one in which many of the boundaries between categories once thought mutually exclusive are weakening and blurring. This book draws on a number of emerging ideas associated with this tendency, including actor–network theory (especially the writings of Bruno Latour), complexity theory, the work of Donna Haraway and the philosophical ideas of Gilles Deleuze. This is not an exhaustive list but represents simply those writers and schools of thought that I have found useful and inspiring in the development of my own thinking. Two common themes are expressed, in different ways, by each of them. These are, first, the heterogeneity (or hybridity) of phenomena and, second, their interconnected, networked and emergent becoming. These themes pervade this book. However, I do not give a comprehensive account of different thinkers' ideas, presented as a theoretical framework at the start. Rather, I draw on them selectively, giving them exposition throughout the book, when it seems timely for the development of my argument.

A crucial implication of the argument that I make in this book is that childhood studies are necessarily an interdisciplinary field. Fortunately, the recognition that childhood studies should be constituted in this way is already gaining ground. It was, for example, the conclusion of a group of childhood scholars at a symposium, organized by Jill Korbin and Rick Settersten, at Case Western Reserve University in Cleveland during July 2003. Constructing such an interdisciplinary field will be a complex business. The prospect raises difficult issues in relation to knowledge, research, teaching and professional practice. At that meeting it was felt that an inter-disciplinary field should be seen as a long-term goal, with the idea of a multi-disciplinary field as a more realistic and achievable immediate aim. As noted above, the new social studies of childhood already includes a multi-disciplinary cast of contributors. However, collaborative exchange so far has generally been limited to the social sciences and, to some extent, the humanities. This is a promising start but the really problematic relationship is between, on the one hand, the natural sciences and, on the other, the social sciences and humanities. This division, expressing the gap between the 'two cultures' that C.P. Snow drew attention to in the mid-twentieth century, creates many obstacles to the possibility of merging perspectives but the future of childhood studies depends upon how it is handled. Every opportunity possible to create and develop a dialogue between the natural, social and human sciences should be taken. Setting out a ground from which those active in the new social studies of childhood might be better able to recognize those opportunities is one of the primary aims of this book.

Alan Prout
Copenhagen, January 2004

1 Changing childhood in a globalizing world

We want to hear the voices of young people, influencing and shaping local services; contributing to their local communities; feeling heard; feeling valued; being treated as responsible citizens

(Children and Young People's Unit, 2000: 27)

Introduction

Towards the end of the twentieth century there developed a pervasive sense that the social order was fragmenting under the pressure of rapid economic, social and technological change. Social theorists expressed this sense of change through terms such as 'late modernity' (Giddens, 1990, 1991) and the 'risk society' (Beck, 1992), arguing that it arose from the destabilization of the institutions holding modern social life together, which altered the bases of identity and meaning. In this chapter I will argue that childhood is also affected by this destabilization. In particular the distinction between adults and children, once firmly established as a feature of modernity, seems to be blurring. Traditional ways of representing childhood in discourse and in image no longer seemed adequate to its emerging forms. New ways of speaking, writing and imaging children are providing new ways of seeing them and these children are different from the innocent and dependent creatures that appeared to populate the first half of the twentieth century. These new representations construct children as more active, knowledgeable and socially participative than older discourses allowed. They are more difficult to manage, less biddable and hence are more troublesome and troubling (Prout, 2000a).

In this chapter I will explore the sources of these shifts in representation, arguing that the modern notion of childhood is changing as the social and economic conditions that produced it, and within which it was implicated, are themselves undergoing significant destabilization. At the centre of this process is an increased awareness of the diversity of childhood. This comes about for two reasons. In the first place the social, cultural and economic conditions within which children live and grow up are increasingly diversified. Second, and just as important, various socio-technical developments in communication have led to a proliferation of images of this diversity. Childhood difference is becoming more visible. This has had paradoxical effects, both homogenizing and differentiating the local construction of childhood and, as a result, fragmenting and undermining once stable notions of what childhood is and what it should be. The heightened interdependencies of the contemporary world mean that the local social and economic conditions of childhood, in the rich countries as well as the poorer ones, are linked by global economic, social, cultural and technological processes.

Childhood and modernity

Contemporary childhood is changing in ways that leave conventional representations of it struggling to capture its new realities. In the rest of this chapter I will explore some of the reasons for this. However, in order to understand what follows, it is first necessary to examine contemporary childhood in its historical context. This context is rooted in the political, economic, technological, social and cultural changes that took place in Europe from about the eighteenth century onwards, which gave rise to the belief that history was entering a distinctive 'modern' era. This complex set of interlocking changes, part material practice and part mode of thought, has come to define what is meant by modernity. In the political sphere it is associated with the rise of the nation state as a territorially bounded unit of sovereignty, within which political power is legitimized by secular rather than religious beliefs and exercised through a complex state bureaucracy.

In economics modernity is associated with the rise of capitalism: the large-scale, industrial production of commodities for the market, on the basis of private property, monetary exchange, and capital accumulation, which came to dominate national and international economic life, gradually displacing or incorporating other economic systems. Associated with this was the decline of traditional social hierarchies, such as those based on feudal rank and their replacement by and incorporation into a new, more dynamic social division of labour. Partly as a consequence of the rise of the nation state and capitalism, new classes and status groups, especially the middle and working classes, began to appear and assume central importance. Traditional relations between the sexes were changed and new forms of gender and sexual relationships developed. New identities were created and contested as urban living allowed new social and cultural possibilities, freeing people from old forms of social control. In 'pre-modern' social formations, change, although sometimes sudden and brutal, was generally slow paced. 'Moderns', in contrast, became accustomed to change that was fast paced, unpredictable and open-ended and, partly as a consequence, a new mentality that orientated to the future was encouraged. Secular and materialist beliefs challenged traditional religious ones and created cultural conditions permeated by rationalist and individualist ideas and values. The Enlightenment championed scientific and rational thought, repositioning nature as a comprehensible and controllable set of resources, and paving the way for the growth of modern technology.

This was the general context within which the modern idea of childhood came into being, although inevitably, when stated this shorthand way, it sounds as if modernity came into being through some homogenous, smooth, uniform and continuous process. In fact it came about through a process that was heterogeneous, uneven, contingent and contested. It took a different form and path according to local circumstances. In some places old forms were often incorporated rather than completely displaced. For example, where France underwent the convulsions of a political revolution, Britain saw the incorporation of parts of the old landed ruling class into the emergence of industrial capitalism. In various places capitalism did not displace other modes of production but enveloped them, so that, for example, the emergence of British capitalism was intimately connected with the expansion of slavery in the Americas. In general, huge social conflicts were generated as groups resisted change or as new antagonisms were created. So, while Britain avoided a political revolution of the type experienced in France, it did experience intense social conflict in the shape of the Chartist movement, the emergence of the trades unions, the struggle for the vote and so on. Furthermore, while the general trend and direction of change was as summarized above, developments in different spheres (the state, the economy, etc.) occurred at different times and under the influence of many different factors which came into play at different times. It is an error, therefore, to treat modernity as reducible, even in the 'last instance', to some single driving force, such as the mode of production in the Marxist schemes of historical development or the inevitable outcome of a hypostatized 'modernization process'. There was no single underlying modernization process that underpinned developments in all places and led inevitably to a single predetermined end point, albeit at different speeds.

As part of this process, unevenly, over a long period and shaped by specific sets of local circumstances a distinctly modern idea of childhood came into existence. Understandings of this process customarily begin with the ground-breaking historical work of Aries (1962). His argument is drawn mostly from French materials but the process he describes has been widely interpreted as common to most European societies. In essence he argues that between the fifteenth and seventeenth centuries a new concept of children arose that paved the way to the modern idea of childhood. In medieval society infants were seen as vulnerable but after the age of about seven or eight children were seen and treated as 'miniature adults'. According to Aries, these changes had three sources. First, was a changing emotional economy of the family, in which children became more valued and more protected. Second, and at a later stage, moralists identified childhood as an immature period, which meant that children were in need of extended discipline and training. Third, schools became age-graded institutions increasingly thought of as the place where children properly belonged.

These changes in belief, and the institutional arrangements through which they were materialized and put into practice, gradually spread through all social classes. Later historians (Cunningham, 1991; Hendrick, 1997a; Heywood, 2001; Pollock, 1983) have critiqued, modified and extended Aries' basic idea, showing how modern childhood was formed through diverse discourses and practices around child labour, criminality and welfare. Cunningham (1991: 7) sums up the process thus:

> between the late seventeenth and mid-twentieth centuries there occurred a major and irreversible change in the representations of childhood, to the point where all children throughout the world were thought to be entitled to certain common elements and rights of childhood.

There is, however, a tendency towards essentialism in Aries' account that can produce problems parallel to those found in the disappearance of childhood literature (see pp. 14–15). Archard (1993) discusses this as the problem of 'presentism'. Archard rejects the view that because the treatment of children in the past differed from its contemporary version, then it can be concluded that there was no childhood. Rather, modernity produced a particular version of childhood, different in some important respects from that which preceded it and that which might follow. In this sense modernity did not 'invent' or 'discover' childhood. As I will argue in later chapters (especially Chapter 4) there are biological aspects of childhood that are translated into and stand in relation to its discursive dimensions, ensuring that some sort of extended juvenility marks the early period of the human developmental life course. However, modernity's encounter with childhood did bring about a transformation in the way that childhood was understood. Stated briefly one could say that modernity constituted children as the 'cultural other' of adulthood (Christensen, 1994). In particular it put into place a framework of meaning that constituted childhood through a heightened, dichotomized and oppositional relationship between it and adulthood. These oppositions are familiar ones and they include:

Childhood	:	Adulthood
Private	:	Public
Nature	:	Culture
Irrational	:	Rational
Dependent	:	Independent
Passive	:	Active
Incompetent	:	Competent
Play	:	Work

In Chapter 2, I will discuss how such a set of oppositions was implicated in the creation and development of childhood studies. However, the theme of oppositional dichotomies, and their apparently increasing inability to provide a framework for understanding contemporary childhood, runs throughout the whole of this book. The nub of my argument is that childhood studies must take a step from this modernist conception, if they are to become closer to the open-ended, interdisciplinary form of enquiry necessary to present-day conditions.

Childhood representations

As a first step in that argument I will first examine how contemporary childhood is changing and, because we live in a world that increasingly deals in visual imagery, I will begin with the issue of childhood representation in pictures. In an important study, Higonnet (1998) examines how children have been painted and photographed from the eighteenth century to the present. She shows how romantic representations of childhood, such as those found in the paintings of Reynolds and Gainsborough, were constructed through a semiotic opposition with adulthood. They project a vision of childhood that is defined strongly by what it is not. The childhood represented in such images is innocent because it does not, except by omission, refer to the bodies of adult pleasure. These pictures extract childhood from social life, Higonnet argues, because they tell no stories of adult life and its categories of social difference. They efface class and gender, presenting innocent children in the social limbo that was the 'secret garden' of idealized childhood.

Such images were popularized and widely diffused by both the artistic and commercial branches of illustration during the nineteenth and twentieth century. They are still with us. Although images of children virtually disappeared from modernist art of the twentieth century, the romantic legacy lives on in the images still used on birthday cards, biscuit tins and in the sort of advertising that wishes to convey a sense of unproblematic family life. It forms the essential template for the mid-twentieth-century family snapshot. Such imagery is concerned with maintaining the boundary between childhood and adulthood. It is part of a discourse in which childhood, as Holland (1992: 14) puts it, 'as well as being different from adulthood, is its obverse, a depository of many precious qualities adulthood needs but cannot tolerate as part of itself'. Such images of romantic childhood project and imply the idea of childhood's natural state: childhood as a time of innocence, free of cares and responsibilities.

But by the final decades of the twentieth century the domination of this sentimental ideal was under challenge. Victorian and Edwardian images of children, such as those created by the Reverend Dodgson, were being scrutinized (and denounced) for their now apparent sexual preoccupation. A well known TV newsreader in the UK was threatened with prosecution after an employee in a photo-processing laboratory reported that she had taken pictures of her children naked. In the US the Director of the Cincinnati Contemporary Arts Center was charged (though later acquitted) with 'pandering obscenity' after staging an exhibition of controversial photographs by the artist Robert Mablethorpe, some of which were of children.

These are merely the highly publicized tip of a much bigger iceberg. Less sensational but, perhaps, ultimately more important were new styles of photographing children identified by Higonnet:

> In every branch of the media, whether ostensibly commercial or artistic, new images of childhood are appearing. The children represented in these new images are much more physical and challenging than the ones Romantic imagery accustomed us to, so much so that the entire Romantic definition of childhood is being called into question.
>
> (Higonnet, 1998: 107).

In these contemporary images issues of gender, class, poverty, ethnicity and family life are signalled and (sometimes) confronted. The children are diverse. They are sometimes victims but they are also victors. They have emotional range. They are active, aware, judgemental and complex. As Higonnet rightly concludes, a new version of childhood is here being fabricated. It is a construction to be found in many examples of popular culture, including films such as *Look Who's Talking* (in which toddlers are literally 'given a voice' to comment on and act in the social world). As Christensen (1999: 6–7) notes:

> The central plot of all these productions is the constant contrast made between the world of children (and young people) and the adult world. Traditional (op)positions and commonly perceived conflicts of every-day family life get highlighted by twisting around 'child' and 'adult' power, control, competence and responsibility and by exaggerating elements of these dichotomous relationships. Such depictions often portray the embarrassing, weak and preposterous adult in relation to the lively, clever and smart child or demonstrate the adults' shortcomings when confronted with children's manipulative powers and alternative worldviews. The fictional representation of familial combats and their arbitrary solutions tend to favour children over adults and allows qualities such as logic and power to be dislodged from their usual site in the adult.

Usually, as Christensen also notes, this is a temporary reversal and the story line returns children and adults to their conventional roles and positions but, nevertheless, the possibility of slippage between child and adult has been dramatically opened up.

Images of global childhood

Images of active, canny, competent children are, however, but one of a multiplicity of childhood representations conveyed by the contemporary mass media. Although some of these repeat earlier sentimentalized versions, among this kaleidoscope of childhood representations are ones that forcibly remind the viewer that ideal childhood is unevenly distributed across the world. The consumers of images of children in distress are mostly located in the wealthy regions of the world but the children represented in them are not. While poverty, exploitation and malnutrition are to be found outside South America, Asia and Africa, it is these places that are most often represented through pictures of unhappy, hungry, exhausted and exploited children.

Images of the child victims of famine, natural disaster, poverty, war, burdensome work and cruelty have ambiguous effects. Their purpose is to make an emotionally powerful appeal to the rich, or the relatively rich, for financial aid, appealing to their consciences in the hope of credit card donations. However, in evoking the pity of the wealthy they also reinforce their sense of superiority. Hence non-governmental organizations (NGOs) and others wage their campaign against 'aid fatigue', insisting on 'positive images' and struggling to show the determination, knowledge and energy with which children (and adults) confront their situations. Images of suffering children also underline an important element of the idealized discourse of childhood: these children exemplify the vulnerability and dependence that are projected as the natural state of childhood. At the same time they confront the viewer with the gap between the idealized image of childhood and the harsh realities of life for most of the world's children.

In writing about the vast disparities between poor and rich children in Brazil, Goldstein (1998) comments that childhood in Brazil is a privilege of the rich and is practically non-existent for the poor. In a sense this is true. Rich Brazilian children share the same kind of experiences as many children in the developed world. For example, they attend school (or receive other forms of education) and their involvement in paid labour or the domestic economy is limited. In contrast, for many poor Brazilian children schooling is limited and for some non-existent, and they are expected to contribute to the family economy through domestic work and paid labour. Some are cut adrift from their families, living as 'street children'. But to say that these poor children do not have a childhood is a highly normative statement. It is to naturalize the childhood of the rich as the only form that childhood can take. It turns it into a 'gold standard' against which all others are to be judged and (usually) found wanting. In short it essentializes childhood and identifies it with one socially and historically located construction.

This is not at all to deny that poor children in Brazil and elsewhere do not need urgent improvements in their social and economic conditions.

They, and the adults with whom they share their lives, are undoubtedly suffering from all kinds of severe privation. However, their lives also teach us that, in struggling to understand childhood, we need to keep the question of what childhood is open. If the question is closed too soon then we run the risk of concluding the majority of the world's children do not 'have a childhood'. What seems more useful is to accept what images of global childhood forcefully speak of: that there is a great deal of diversity in how childhood is constituted between and within societies, and that it is influenced no less than adulthood by the differences that cleave social life.

The disappearance of childhood

The same conclusion can also be drawn from a third instance of childhood's crisis of representation at the end of the twentieth century. In the wealthy countries of the North (especially the US) the last decades of the twentieth century saw a proliferation of texts (Elkind, 1981; Postman, 1983; Steinberg and Kincheloe 1997; Winn, 1984) announcing the 'disappearance of childhood'. These writers challenged newly emerging constructs of childhood by questioning their ontological status. They interpret late-twentieth-century change in childhood as a sign that childhood as a social institution is in the process not merely of changing but of disappearing. Appalled at the breakdown of the boundary between adulthood and childhood, which they regard as historically progressive and even necessary, they point the finger of blame at technological innovations such as TV and the internet. These, they argue, are leading to the disappearance of childhood by making a wider range of information available to children.

The claim that childhood is disappearing finds resonance in all kinds of wider public debates and concerns. For example, many children are under increasing pressure to succeed in schooling systems that subject them to testing regimes and examinations at an ever earlier age and to many critics it appears that the secret garden of childhood has been transformed into a hot-house. Cultural changes that have, in some degree at least, rendered parent–child relations more open and democratic are frequently deplored because they are seen as reducing the control and supervision of children by adults. The destabilization of family life, common through the industrial and post-industrial world, is often condemned as changing the life circumstances of many children. For these reasons the idea of 'disappearing childhood' has a certain popular appeal. However, on the other side of this discussion are commentators who also hail the social, and especially technological, change that they too see as undermining the adult–child distinction. These writers, however, valorize the advent of the 'electronic generation' as the bearers of progress, welcoming information technology in all its forms as unambiguously reversing generational hierarchies and liberating children from out-dated social forms:

Not only is this new machinery making the young more sophisticated, altering their ideas of what culture and literacy are, it is transforming them – connecting them with one another, providing a new sense of political self . . . children can for the first time reach past the suffocating boundaries of social convention, past their elders' rigid notions of what is good for them.

(Katz, 1997 : 173–4)

Children, then, are seen here as the vanguard of a new digital society.

The factors identified by writers on both side of this debate do indeed have important implications for childhood (see Chapter 5). However, I do not share their mutual (but differently valued) conclusion that childhood is disappearing. Rather, I concur with Buckingham (2000) in his trenchant critique of the excesses of 'death of childhood' literature when he writes that:

Both positions adopt an essentialist view of 'childhood' and 'youth', and an unduly deterministic account of the role of the media and technology. Both reflect a kind of sentimentality about children and young people which fails to acknowledge the diversity of the lived experience of childhood.

(Buckingham, 2000: 57)

One side of the debate is an expression of a deep cultural conservativism that misapprehends change as decay (or even extinction). Such thinking tends to be suffused with a nostalgic longing for childhood to remain the same – or, more usually, to stay as it is imagined to have been in the 1950s. On the other is a wildly exaggerated assessment of the effects of information and communication technology, which among other problems simply ignores how unevenly distributed is the access to it by children in different social and economic circumstances. Their views are by turns technophobic or technophiliac, and are in both cases alloyed with a crude technological determinism that posits a straightforward, one-way influence between technology and social relations.

Globalization and childhood

Shifts in the character of contemporary childhood are, however, more than representational. If the available representations of childhood seem to be less and less adequate then this is in part because their referent is also changing. The conditions that sustained those formerly dominant images of childhood, and which were able successfully to manage the tension between them and their referents, are changing. Holding together the modern representations of childhood and the changing phenomena to which they are supposed to refer is becoming more and more difficult, to the extent that it can no longer be accomplished in a more or less convincing way.

These problems are, in part, a product of the period of intensified social and economic change that started during the last thirty or forty years of the twentieth century and continues today. The dynamic of this social change can be traced to the processes that have created 'globalization'. Before examining this point in more detail it is necessary to sound a warning about the dangers of employing abstractions such as globalization. Like the term 'modernization', pointing to 'globalization' does not in itself provide an explanation of social and economic trends, it merely summarizes and gathers together a set of phenomena under a single convenient heading. Once we ask questions about what globalization consists of and how it comes into being then it appears as a complex and heterogeneous phenomenon. To put the consequence of this position in its most minimal way one could say that globalization has both economic and cultural aspects. On the economic front, it is clear that globalization is not an entirely new phenomenon. Since its mercantile form in fifteenth-century Europe, capitalism has involved the tendency to expand internationally in the search for new markets. In doing so it has absorbed existing non-capitalist economies. In the eighteenth and nineteenth centuries it integrated slavery and in the twentieth century it has penetrated and combined with the Chinese economy, producing a hybrid of centralized state control with rapid marketization. In general, however, once capitalist economic relationships enter a local economy they erode and eventually shatter existing production systems and consumption patterns, pulling them into an increasingly internationalized set of relationships. This was the picture through most of the nineteenth and twentieth centuries when the world market was created and consolidated.

Economic globalization

Globalization theories argue that these tendencies have now been taken a step further, claiming that the world economy is, or is well on its way to becoming, a single, integrated system. Such a prospect sharply divides political opinion. On one side, that of anti-globalization protesters, a picture is drawn of multinational corporations roaming the world in search of investment opportunities, of unimpeded commerce overriding national boundaries, of production being organized on a 'global assembly line' and of the subordination of local economies to the tutelage of a few corporations based in very rich countries, especially the US. At the other political pole the International Monetary Fund and the World Bank argue that, painful though the process might be, drawing all countries into the world economy will liberate their productive potential and lead to increased wealth and universal prosperity. While there are undoubtedly arguments to be made in both directions, both positions exaggerate the degree to which a single global economy has, for the moment, been brought into existence. In fact the only economic activity that can be said to be completely globalized is the financial sector. Trade relations, although involving a high level of internationalization, do not present a picture of unimpeded commercial flow. Rather, we have seen the emergence of trade blocs (such as the European Union and the North American Free Trade Area) within which trade barriers have been minimized or abolished. Although there is long-term pressure for the reduction of barriers between blocs, they currently seek to protect themselves against rivals, often creating great difficulties for developing countries who are forced to trade on unequal terms.

The trend in the organization of production during the mid-twentieth century was towards the growing domination of multinational enterprises such as General Motors or the Philips electronic group. These firms organized production in many different countries, where they engaged in direct foreign investment. By the end of the 1980s it was estimated that there were some 20,000 such businesses, which taken together accounted for over a quarter of the economic activity of the market economies of the world. Such businesses are certainly still of huge importance in the world economy. However, it is far from clear that there is an inevitable process through which the world economy will become completely dominated by a few corporations based in a handful of rich countries. In the first place direct foreign investment by multinational businesses has been declining since the end of the 1980s. Rather, the end of the twentieth century has seen a diversification and internationalization of multinational enterprises, with a significant number now originating in the oil-producing countries, as well as Asia. Multinational companies are also choosing to avoid the immense cost of managing complex production across the world. Increasingly their strategy is to remain regional but form strategic alliances with other regionally based businesses.

None of this, however, denies the immense economic power of multinationals or the impact they have on ordinary people around the world. It does, however, question the extent to which the world economy is set on an inevitable path to global integration and domination by a few mega-corporations. In fact the share of industrial production in Europe and the US has contracted since 1945. In part this is because industrial production has been dispersed to less-developed countries. Some of these (notably in SE Asia and Latin America) have emerged as 'newly industrializing countries', sometimes with measures of wealth that have overtaken some of the developed market economies. However, it also depends upon whether the concentration of economic power is met with resistance, for example by emergent labour movements, and whether measures to regulate economic activity at a world level are put into place.

The gradients of childhood inequality

Nevertheless, there are vast disparities in the social and economic conditions of children's (and adults') lives around the globe and these are a consequence of the workings of the global economy. According to the United Nation's Children's Fund (UNICEF) 90 per cent of the world's wealth is owned by 10 per cent of the population. The dynamics of this global distribution are such that the world's poorest people are actually getting poorer. In part this is a consequence of the International Monetary Fund and the World Bank who for the last two decades have insisted that the economies of Africa, Asia and South America adopt the free-market policies that were gradually put into place in rich countries following the economic crisis of the 1970s. These policies consist of cutting state expenditure on health, welfare and education, reversing the state ownership of enterprises, and removing or lowering barriers to free trade. Such measures have had an uneven effect, stimulating some economies to growth while trapping others in retrenchment and debt. However, there is no doubting that they have had a very severe impact on the world's poorest people. In the five years between 1988 and 1993 the real income of the world's poorest five per cent actually fell by over a quarter (UNICEF, 1996). In 1990 the annual income per person in high-income countries was 56 times greater than in low-income countries; by 1999 it was 63 times greater (UNICEF, 2001). The number of people struggling to survive on less than $1 per day (the international measure of absolute poverty) rose by ten million for every year of the 1990s.

These inequalities are commonly presented as a cleavage between a set of binary divisions deriving from the international division of labour that characterized the world economy of the mid-twentieth century. A product of economic processes associated with colonialism, the world economy could be divided into the core, metropolitan economies of the United States and Europe, which were based on capital intensive, high value-adding production, and peripheral economies that engaged in labour intensive, low value-adding production. This picture was represented in the shifting language of contrasts between the modern and the traditional, the developed and the underdeveloped, the industrial and the non-industrial, the first and the third worlds, the North and the South, the minority world and the majority. Although this language of binary division dramatically illustrates the inequalities of the situation, it is now too crude a distinction to capture the emerging pattern of an increasingly complex, volatile and unpredictable world economy. There continue to be significant differences between the regions of the world but these cannot be captured in a simple binary division. Not all economic trends are marked by a growing divergence of the richest from the rest. In the 1990s average incomes rose in Latin America, the Caribbean, the Middle East and North Africa. Until the financial crash of 1997, East Asia saw rapid economic growth and some countries have recovered quickly. China is the world's fastest growing economy, which in 2003 is predicted to achieve a growth rate of 8.5 per cent. It will overtake both Britain and France to become the world's fourth biggest economy well before the end of 2005. While the rural population of China has income levels below the poverty line, the average disposable income in towns and cities – home to two-fifths of China's 1.3bn people – rose by nine per cent in the first nine months of 2003. By way of contrast, in the former countries of the Soviet and Eastern bloc, the transition to market economies has resulted in higher unemployment and massive social dislocation, while social spending has declined and the social safety net has been eroded. Despite its record of economic growth, the Indian sub-continent has experienced growing inequality. Most disturbing of all, very few countries of Sub-Saharan Africa experienced any rise in incomes at all and most saw incomes shrinking.

It is, of course, difficult to predict what the future of the world economy holds but overall the current picture is of a global gradient rather than a binary economic division. This gradient is further reflected in inequalities in children's health, welfare and education. For example, the key measure of mortality amongst children under five shows a gradient according to national wealth (UNICEF, 2001: 8):

Lowest wealth quintile: 159 per thousand
Second wealth quintile: 150 per thousand
Middle wealth quintile: 131 per thousand
Fourth wealth quintile: 110 per thousand
Highest wealth quintile: 76 per thousand

However, in line with the effects of world economic policy since the 1980s, underlying this gradient are some growing inequalities. Already experiencing the highest child mortality rates in the world, nine out of fourteen Sub-Saharan countries saw child mortality increase.

A similar gradient can be found for the enrolment of children into primary education. The UNICEF summarizes the situation thus (2001: 56–7):

> The most notable progress has been made in the East Asia and Pacific region, where both the net and the gross enrolment ratios have moved close to 100 per cent in most countries . . . Steady progress in the countries of the Caribbean and Latin America has cut the number of children out of school. Similar progress has occurred for children in the Arab states, although the overall number of out-of-school children has increased. South Asian enrolment increases have barely kept up with the growth in the population of school-age children . . . The region experiencing the least progress, and in some cases actual regression, is sub-Saharan Africa. War and displacement, malnutrition and disease (especially HIV/AIDS) and economic crisis have reduced the availability and quality of education services in a number of countries.

In a globalizing world inequalities have not disappeared, on the contrary they have been intensified. The economic system that once divided the world into rich metropolitan countries and poor peripheral ones is breaking down and this has reinforced some existing inequalities but it has also redistributed poverty and wealth in new ways. Globalization is creating effects that transcend the scale of the national state, wherever it is located on the gradient of the rich and the poor. Frønes (1993, 1997) has argued that one effect of globalization is that childhoods similar to those of the Euro-American middle classes are being produced and distributed around the world. These often appear within the protected enclaves of elites in developing countries such that the childhoods of privileged children in New York and Delhi may have more in common with each other than with the majority in either location. It can be concluded, then, that on a global scale economic and other associated inequalities between children are widening at the extremes. However, they are also diminishing as the stark division between rich metropolitan and poor peripheral countries is replaced by a gradient along which countries, regions, households and individuals are distributed according to how well they have fared in the new economic conditions of the world economy.

Childhood poverty in the rich countries

These global economic trends also affect the richest countries, creating both greater wealth and more inequality within national economies. Capitalism in its imperialist form created conditions that sheltered sections of the metropolitan working class. In part this consisted of the concentration of industrial production in the metropolitan countries, creating employment which to a significant extent has now been exported to the less developed and newly industrializing countries. This has led to the creation of the 'rust-belt' enclaves of high unemployment and social decay that became a feature of European and North American societies in the 1980s and 1990s. As a consequence of this and other longer-term trends to de-industrialization, the majority of employment in the metropolitan economies is now concentrated in the service sector. But not all service sector employment is equal. There is a gradient from the well-paid professional and technical careers of the 'knowledge economy' to the badly paid, insecure menial jobs in the 'hamburger-flipping' sectors.

The metropolitan working class also enjoyed the benefits of the welfare states that they struggled to establish during the twentieth century. These too give significant benefits and protection against the risks of the market economy. The form of this welfare capitalism varied from country to country. Esping-Andersen (1990) provides a basis for comparing and contrasting different regimes by describing three ideal types of welfare state: the conservative corporatist (for example, Germany), the neo-liberal (for example, the UK) and the social democratic (for example, Sweden). Each regime is understood as a constellation of social, political and economic arrangements which cultivate a particular variety of welfare system, which in turn supports a particular pattern of stratification. At the core of Esping-Andersen's analysis is the concept of de-commodification. This refers to a service or benefit being available as a matter of right, such that people can maintain a livelihood without reliance on the market. It indicates, therefore, the extent to which the welfare state modifies the centrality of capitalism as the dominant force shaping everyday lives.

Esping-Andersen's analysis has been criticized in a number of ways (see Pringle, 1998). The rather static character of his typology gives it only limited value in discussing the dynamics of welfarism. Like all typologies it groups together cases that are different in significant ways: for example, Denmark is not Norway and Italy and Germany have many social, cultural and economic differences. Although it is focused on the rich part of the world, especially the 'modern' societies of Europe and North America, it is not comprehensive even in these terms. It misses out countries such as Greece, Portugal and Ireland, and all of the countries of the former communist bloc. Other analysts have, controversially, added the category of 'rudimentary' welfare regimes to cover the first case and attempts have been made to analyse the rather uncertain and disparate trends in eastern Europe, not to mention those of South America and Asia.

However, all forms of the welfare state have, over the last few decades, come under increasing pressure to retrench. As Esping-Andersen (1996: 25) comments:

> There is a seemingly universal trade-off between equality and employment. Its roots may lie primarily in the new world order, but our study identifies significantly different national responses. Within the group of advanced welfare states, only a few have undertaken radical steps to roll back or deregulate the existing system. All, however, have sought to trim benefits at the margin or to introduce more cautious measures of flexibilization ... [T]hose following a more radical liberalization strategy do better in terms of employment but suffer a high cost in terms of inequality and poverty. In contrast, those resilient to change pay the price of high unemployment – continental Europe in particular.

Although all this has taken place against a background of generally rising living standards, there is also evidence for an increasing differentiation between those who share most in growing affluence and those who have benefited least.

This has had a particular impact on children. A recent study based on OECD data asked whether income distribution between children is becoming more unequal within industrialized countries. It appears that it is. Of the 17 countries included in the study 12 of them showed growing income inequality between children (Oxley *et al.*, 2001: 378). International comparison of trends in child poverty presents a complex picture and is subject to many methodological difficulties. Nevertheless, a recent analysis of Luxembourg Income Study data suggests that during the last quarter-century the proportion of children in families with less than 50 per cent of median income rose in 11 of the 20 countries studied. These included Australia, Belgium, Germany, Italy, the Netherlands, the UK and the US (Bradshaw, 2000: 240). Although growing inequality can be seen across the whole range of welfare regimes it is especially in the neo-liberal ones that child poverty is most on the increase. This suggests that even though the rise in child poverty can be ultimately traced back to world economic trends, some societies have welfare regimes and policies in place that have protected children, while others, in varying degrees, do not. The UK between 1980 and 1995 is a clear example of a country that allowed the general rise in poverty and inequality to fall disproportionately on children.

The effects of child poverty have long been studied by social scientists through cross-sectional and longitudinal surveys. These studies usually examine the relationship between growing up in poverty and various outcomes in later life. A recent systematic review of the evidence in the UK (Bradshaw, 2001) concluded that there is good evidence to show that poor children experience higher levels of mortality, illness, fatal accidents, neglect and physical abuse, poor housing and homelessness, teenage pregnancy, smoking, suicide and mental illness. Their educational attainment is also lower. Another recent study (Hobcraft, 1998) analysed longitudinal data from the UK National Child Development Study, to examine whether 'social exclusion' (a somewhat wider concept than poverty) is transmitted across the generations. Its general conclusion was that:

> there is little doubt that social exclusion, as captured by the adult outcomes and childhood factors used here, is transmitted across the generations and through the life-course. There is also little doubt that there are a large number of very specific continuities from childhood experience into adulthood.
>
> (Hobcraft, 1998: 100)

The study tells a story familiar from earlier studies of poverty in childhood coupled with low parental interest in education, producing low attainment at school and reproducing low income in adulthood. Studies of children's own experiences of poverty, of what they mean for their own childhood and how they contribute to their characteristic ways of seeing the world, are much rarer. Ridge (2002), however, has presented just such a picture of how contemporary (English) life looks from the perspective of poor children and how it permeates many different, and sometimes unexpected, aspects of their lives. She advocates that policy makers pay much greater attention to these voices.

Within the Anglo-American social sciences there is a long-standing and unresolved debate about the effect on children's development of being brought up in a single-parent household. This might in a large measure be thought to reflect those societies' ideological obsession with women who do not conform to expected patterns of marriage and child-bearing. Certainly a different view is taken in the Scandinavian countries, where the research interest in this topic is much more muted. However, one of the many problems of interpreting the available evidence is that it is very difficult to disentangle 'family factors' from those of poverty. Low income, for example, is both a consequence of divorce or separation and a precursor of it. A recent study (Joshi *et al.*, 1999) looking at data from the UK and the US traced the separate influence of these factors. It concluded that social disadvantage, especially where it is long standing, is more important than the form of children's family in shaping their educational and behavioural outcomes. This remains a controversial area but, whatever research may conclude, it serves to remind us that alongside growing economic inequality, contemporary childhood is also shaped by changes in the family.

The family in late modernity

Feminist critiques (for example, Lewis, 1992) of Esping-Andersen's typology criticize its starting point in the idea of de-commodification, arguing that this embodies a specifically male point of view, derived from the 'public' sphere of paid work and class relations. In doing so it neglects the 'private' sphere of the family and domestic work, which is a large sector of already decommodified activity. On this basis feminists have argued for an alternative way of looking at welfare states as expressions of their relationship to the assumptions of a 'male bread-winner' model society. Welfare regimes vary according to the extent to which they assume the existence of unpaid caring work, frequently carried out by women, or whether this is 'substituted' by services such as childcare. Creighton (1999), for example, discusses the UK in these terms, suggesting that its welfare regime has made only a partial transition from one in which unpaid caring work was assumed, to one in which such services are widely available. He points out, for example, that childcare services are not sufficient to support families in which both marital partners work, a situation which can be contrasted with the much more extensive network of childcare found in the Nordic countries.

As already noted economic policies since the 1970s have emphasized de-regulation and labour market flexibility, and alongside this unemployment, part-time employment and job insecurity have grown. Euro-American economies have shifted from industrial service sector employment, a trend that has accompanied the increased participation of women in the labour market. This change in the gender composition of the working population has been a key economic shift since the mid-twentieth century, such that the assumption, widely accepted before the Second World War, that the main breadwinner for a family would be the father/husband, while the mother/wife would look after the home has to a significant degree disappeared. This has had implications not only for the economic situation of families and their patterns of income and spending but has also altered the texture of everyday family life. This has changed the experience of children, who are now likely to experience the home as a place of 'comings and going' (Christensen *et al.*, 2000). Although the evidence does not support the claim that children and parents spend less time together, it is true that (in the UK at least) both experience a 'time squeeze' (Christensen, 2002). Contemporary families have to engage with complex timetables in order to coordinate the activities of its different members, both adults and children. Indeed, it has been suggested (Prout, 2003) that part of the appeal of the idea of children as active and socially participative can be traced to the obvious advantages that such children would have in the everyday management of household timetables.

It appears, then, that economic changes such as the flexibilization of production, the decline of old patterns of employment and the emergence of new ones have had an effect on the families of which children are members. These, however, are part of a wider transformation in which economically driven change is paralleled by multi-dimensional social and cultural changes affecting a wide range of relationships and spheres: class, gender, ethnicity, identity, ecological and risk awareness, and practices in civil society and politics. As a result the core institutions of modernity, which characterized industrial societies for most of the twentieth century, have been 'disembedded' and 'hollowed out' (Giddens, 1990, 1991). A key example of this is the fragmentation of family forms, which have greatly diversified the circumstances within which children grow up, especially when family change is associated with poverty. Patterns of household formation and maintenance established in industrialized societies during the nineteenth and early twentieth centuries have been shattered and replaced by a new pluralism. There are differences but the overall trend and general direction is the same in the US and Europe (Clarke, 1996; Ruxton, 1996; US Department of Health and Human Resources, 1998). Both have seen a steady demographic decline in the nuclear family. This is itself the product of a number of linked trends in population and household formation. These include a decline in the number of marriages and a rise in the number of divorces; an increase in cohabitation, an increase in extra-marital births, and the growth in stepfamilies and lone-parent families.

Demographers and sociologists find it increasingly difficult to categorize the complex new family forms that are emerging from these processes. But this is not just a problem of academic classification. Ordinary people share it, as they struggle to name and adapt to complex new sets of kinship and quasi-kinship relationships that emerge from family change. Sirota (2001, 2002), for example, has been carrying out an ongoing study of French children's birthday parties. It shows how families patch together a *bricolage* of practices and rules concerning who is (and is not) invited to the party, a problem created by the intricate network of new relationships that emerges from (sometimes multiple) divorce and remarriage. Simpson (1998) refers to this as the shift from the nuclear to the 'unclear family', commenting that the mid-twentieth century may have seen a zenith in family stability that is now, perhaps, entering a period of instability (see also Seccombe, 1993). In the main, Simpson documents the implication of divorce and separation of the adults involved. However, he also notes the way in which the unclear family raises questions about the boundary between adulthood and childhood:

> The child no longer occupies a single location within the life cycle but might well end up managing multiple locations simultaneously as each parent brings into play different constructions of personhood and agency . . . Given the right conditions a child can develop a level of social and practical competence which would be difficult to emulate in a traditional family setting. Children have to develop abilities to manage diverse social settings and develop skills in diplomacy, confidentiality, discretion and tact in dealing with parents.
>
> (Simpson, 1998: 76–7)

While these examples of changing family forms reflect the interplay of economic, social and cultural forces, economic globalization also enters more directly into some forms of family life. While finance flows more or less freely across national borders, labour has to make the same journey in an embodied, material form. Hochschild (2001) has recently argued that this is creating a 'global care chain' that spans the world as the richer employ those poorer to carry out childcare. She describes one common form of this chain:

> [global care chains] often connect three sets of caretakers – one cares for the migrant's children back home, the second cares for the children of the woman who cares for the migrant's children, and a third, the migrating mother herself, cares for the children of the professionals of the First World. Poorer women raise children for wealthier women while still poorer women – or older or more rural – women raise their children.
>
> (Hochschild, 2001: 136)

Hochschild cites an example (taken from the work of Parrenas, 2001) of one mother, Vicky Diaz, a former teacher and travel agent who migrated to the US to work as a nanny for a rich family in Beverly Hills. She did this to raise the money necessary for her own children to be able to attend school. Her own children constantly try to persuade her to return home, creating intense emotional tensions as she is compelled to withhold her care from them but give it to an American child.

Demographic trends in childhood

Shifts in patterns of family formation, domestic life and patterns of work in Europe and North America are also associated with a declining birth rate. Taken together the countries of the European Union now have fertility rates below the threshold of generational replacement. As a result it has been projected that in Europe by 2025 the numbers in the 0–19 age group will fall by over ten per cent (European Commission, 1996). While levels of fertility in the United States are generally higher than those in Europe, the general trend towards lower birth rates is also found. The fertility rate dropped dramatically between 1960 and 1980, when it settled to a level that, with some fluctuations, has more or less remained (Ruxton, 1996; US Department of Health and Human Resources, 1998: 27). A result of this trend is that in both Europe and the US children constitute a declining proportion of the population. It is as yet unclear what the implications of this are for children. However, some social policy analysts have argued that we have seen, and will see a further, redistribution of social resources away from children towards the elderly. This raises important issues about how justice in the distribution of resources between the generations can be achieved and maintained (Sgritta, 1994: 361; Thompson, 1989).

However, although declining birth rates are a worldwide phenomenon, there is great diversity in patterns of population distribution between countries. It is estimated (Population Reference Bureau, 2003) that there were almost two billion children (under the age of 15) on the planet. Overall they represent 30 per cent of the world population. But this proportion varies greatly according to the country and region being considered. At the extremes, in West and East Africa children are 45 per cent of the population, while in the countries of southern Europe, which are experiencing historically low fertility rates, they are a mere 17 per cent of the population, a proportion already exceeded by that of the elderly. In between these extremes other regions and countries form a gradient. The much-heralded world 'population explosion' is in fact confined to the developing countries of Africa, Asia and Latin America, where 97 per cent of the world increase in population is taking place. This expansion is caused by steadily declining mortality rates, especially infant mortality rates. Nevertheless, underlying this growth in population is a worldwide, but uneven, fall in fertility. The standard demographic assumption is that fertility rates in developing countries will continue to decline if education levels rise, populations continue to urbanize and if contraception is increasingly available and practised. This overall trend, however, varies greatly by country. In some, such as Uganda, fertility has not begun to fall. In others, such as Bangladesh, it has fallen but levelled out at a moderately high level. In Iran the fall has been swift and dramatic. Predicting if, when, how far and how fast fertility will fall remains a problematic task.

Transnational migration

Another source of diversity is migration. This is often thought of as a feature of contemporary globalization but in fact mass population movements are much more associated with the early rise of capitalism. Much of it was forced migration in the form of the transatlantic slave trade. Later waves included European migration to the US in the late-nineteenth and early-twentieth centuries and the settlement of British colonies, especially Australasia. By the 1970s tightened immigration controls had slowed the flow of world migrants but, although international statistics are not really adequate to the task of characterizing these flows, it seems that migration is once again on the increase. According to the UN, between 1965 and 1990 the total number of migrants in the developed countries increased nine-fold (ILO, 2003: 26). The pace of increase in the world stock of migrants is also increasing, from 1.2 per cent in 1965–75 to 2.6 per cent in 1985–95 (ILO, 2003: 26). Much of this is in the form of illegal economic migration, such as that from Mexico to the United States, when individual determination overcomes even the most robust attempts of the nation state to restrict it.

Such migration is not only the result of underdevelopment but also of the economic development currently taking place in many newly industrializing economies (Massey, 1998). A cycle occurs in which the migration of men from a poor community creates job opportunities for more women in local industries, which in turn creates the economic possibility of another person making the trip to the rich countries. But in fact many of the world's migrants are women. For example, according to Hochschild (2001: 131) half of the legal migrants from Mexico to the United States were women with a median age of 29, fitting the profile of those involved in the global care chain. As she notes, there is a connection between the post-1945 entry of women into the labour market in the rich countries and the global care chain discussed above.

Migration also has direct implications for the diversification of childhood. At one end of the chain, in the poor countries, there is children's experiences of labour, work poverty, absent parents, insecurity, war, disaster and racism. At the other there is the particular, and often difficult, experience of migrant children in their new host countries. A recent study (Rutter and Candappa, 1998) of refugee children in the UK, based on the children's own accounts, reported their experiences, which included overt racism as well as a more subtle process, such as a lack of concern for their cultural values, through which social exclusion could occur. The study also provided a comparison of refugee children's daily lives, highlighting differences from other children. For example, refugee children acted as translators and mediators for other family members, they contributed more to the domestic work of their households and they had little contact with wider kin, usually because they had left them behind in the country from which they had fled. The research, however, also pointed up the children's endurance through war, flight and displacement, demonstrating their courage and resilience.

Migration is also leading to the growth in racial and ethnic diversity among children in both Europe and the US, a trend that is set to continue over the next decades (Commission of the European Community, 2001; Federal Interagency Forum on Child and Family Statistics, 1999: 5). This trend has implications for the diversity of childhood, children's lived experience and the formation of their identity (Connolly, 1998). Perhaps because of the greater social and political significance of ethnicity in the US, and its overlap with issues of equity and social class, childhood research there has paid greater attention to children's ethnicity. García-Coll *et al.* (2004, forthcoming), for example, have shown the high level of awareness of ethnic categories at a young age and how children develop increasingly sophisticated, elaborate and creative ways of registering their complex identities. The research on 'transnational childhoods' carried out by Thorne and her colleagues in California addresses the local implications of this complexity and mobility (Thorne, 2004, forthcoming; Orellana *et al.*, 1998, 2001). It shows, for example, that some children routinely move back and forth over national boundaries, forming and reforming, joining and separating from households both in the US and in another country. Again, in local contexts children's experience of ethnic difference becomes played out in unpredictable ways through children's own creative practices.

Childhood and cultural globalization

Children's engagement in processes of ethnic identification underline the more widespread fragmentation of identity that is a characteristic of a globalizing world. In late modernity the sources of social diversity have been broadened and complicated. If modernity was most overtly concerned with social class and its politics organized around party and state forms, then late modernity has added many other dimensions of difference. Gender, ethnicity, disability, family structure, sexual orientation, generational position, life course trajectory, lifestyle and consumption all provide the diverse materials with which identity is formed and its social and political correlates practised.

Although, as I have suggested above, a fully globalized world economy does not yet exist, there are some economic activities that do take place in a truly integrated world system. They are concentrated in those areas of the economy which are concerned with symbolic production and exchange. For example, the world finance system is a more or less fully globalized part of the world economy. This is largely because new socio-technical systems of communication have been developed that make possible the more or less instantaneous transfer of capital. Partly as a consequence and partly as a condition for its very possibility, finance capital has been able to assume a symbolic form. Money transfers take the form of electronic flows through circuits rather than movements of cash in their traditional metallic or paper forms.

This runs alongside what Lash and Urry (1994) term the 'dematerialization' of production. In part this phenomenon concerns the expanded production of symbolic products. These images and representations take many forms, including mass media products such as TV, the cinema and the internet. In this respect the term dematerialization might be questioned because the circuits that bring together power stations, electrical grids, optical fibre, electrons, satellites, computer screens and computers are no less material than the books and newspapers that preceded them. What is different is not the materiality of the flows but the speed and ease of communication and the compression of time and space that this brings about. Through these effects a vast plurality of images, information, ideas and values are disseminated and communicated at high speed and on a global scale.

Such global products and communication processes have paradoxical effects, bringing about both cultural homogenization and differentiation. They connect the local and the global, making the same beliefs and values, for example in liberal democracy or fundamentalist religious belief, available everywhere. In doing so they expand the possibility of what an individual in any locality might choose to accept and engage with in the production of their local meanings. They therefore also expand the possibilities of cultural syncretism and hybridity of identity and of meaning. Their carriage of plurality nurtures relativism, compelling one community of belief to acknowledge the existence of the others. That recognition, however, can entail opposition and hatred and not only tolerance. For example, both fundamentalist American Christian evangelicalism and Islamic militancy employ the mechanisms of global communication. Each can be (partially) understood as fabricated as reactions to the relativism that global culture carries into even the most remote localities.

All of this serves to remind us that the twentieth-century notion of society, as a distinct, bounded entity is in decline. The processes of cultural globalization mean that societies are less and less able to secure their increasingly porous boundaries. They increasingly adopt a lower-level defensiveness that seeks merely to regulate and moderate the powerful new flows of the people, information and products that penetrate and traverse them (Urry, 2000). These transnational mobilities involve information, values and images that most children routinely engage with in one way or another (Buckingham, 2000) and have the paradoxical effects on them that are to be expected from cultural globalization. Looked at from a global perspective childhood culture is becoming more homogenized as the same products, for example toys, games and clothes, become available everywhere.

However, in any one particular location childhood experience becomes more diverse because the range of products is enlarged, thus producing new cultural niches and leading to the emergence of new identities.

Such transnational flows also have profound implications for children's socialization. In fact, for some time now contemporary social science has recognized the increasing complexity of the socialization processes that occur when young children begin to spend a large part of their daily life away from the family – at school, in after-school clubs or in day-care institutions. In the Nordic countries, where these new institutions proliferated in the wake of the Second World War, this gave rise to the idea of 'double social-ization'. The German educationalist Giesecke (1985), however, has suggested that we now also have to acknowledge that children, like adults, live in a pluralistic society. A range of competing, complementary and divergent values and perspectives from parents, school, the media, the consumer society and their peer relations confronts them. He suggests that parents, teachers and other people with responsibility for the care of children have less power to control and steer these different factors as a whole. It becomes, therefore, important to understand children as individually and collectively trying to make coherence and sense of the world in which they live (Christensen and Prout, 2004, forthcoming).

Childhood and individualization

Is it these processes that lie behind the emergence of the 'new child', the child who is self-regulating, active and socially participative? This certainly is the conclusion of the German sociologist Ulrich Beck. He writes that young people:

> no longer become individualized. They individualize themselves. The 'biographization' of youth means becoming active, struggling and designing one's own life.
>
> (Beck, 1998: 78)

As this process of the young being recognized as having 'a life of their own' continues so the more traditional integuments of childhood become increas-ingly strained. According to Beck the logic of the process he terms 'individualization' requires new kinds of institutions in which authority, and allegiance, must be constantly renegotiated, re-established and earned. A recent survey of children's values showed exactly such an attitude on the part of young people (Holland and Thomson, 1999: 3):

> Authority has been described as legitimate power: power that needs not explain or defend itself. There are few figures or institutions other than parents and families that are able to claim such authority in the

eyes of young people. Rather authority has to be earned and negotiated. Young people articulated an 'ethic of reciprocity' arguing that
their respect could be won by anyone who respected them . . . They
tended to be very wary of claims to authority and respect on the basis
of tradition, custom or force.

Children's rights

It was noted above that the processes of cultural globalization both homogenize and differentiate. This is very clearly shown in the emergence
of the global children's rights movement. In 1924 the League of Nations
promulgated the first international agreement setting out the principles
which should inform the universal treatment of children. The underlying
image of the child contained in the Declaration of Geneva was thoroughly
imbued with a modernist concept of childhood. In particular children were
seen as incomplete, non-social, weak and dependent. The Declaration,
therefore, placed its emphasis on the duties of adults towards children. The
UN Convention of the Rights of the Child (UNCRC), agreed in 1989,
took this a stage further by making its provisions legally binding on national
governments that ratified it. By 2003 this included all governments of the
world except the US. The UNCRC, however, surpasses the modernist
notion of children as a cultural other. It raises children's social participation
as a goal alongside protection and provision. Children's participation has
become an international rallying point for child advocacy. It is seen as
capable of transcending differences in the social, cultural and economic
conditions of children's lives around the world (Davie, Upton and Varma,
1996; Flekkoy and Kaufman, 1997; Franklin, 1995; Hart, 1992; Lansdown,
1995).

From one point of view the UNCRC represents a benign attempt to
bring enlightenment and humane standards to all children. It has been used
in this way and it is on these grounds that it draws enthusiastic support and
even evokes a certain amount of zealotry. It has also been characterized as
high in rhetoric but low in intensity. In this sense it is a highly suitable
instrument through which declarations of lofty principle can be made but
about which little needs to be done in practice. However, it is also the case
that the children's rights lobby is, for good or ill, on the forefront of the
global spread of norms about childhood. As Boyden (1997: 197) notes, these
efforts have their precursors in the 'civilizing mission' of colonialism:

> As the twentieth century has progressed, then, highly selective, stereo-
> typical perceptions of childhood – of the innocent child victim on the
> one hand and the young deviant on the other – have been exported
> from the industrial world to the South . . . It has been the explicit goal
> of children's rights specialists to crystallize in international law a
> universal system of rights for the child based on these norms.

The effects of this, she argues, are not always positive. Rights is a concept which is ultimately tied up with cultural values. Their successful implementation depends upon the existence of a compatible framework of meaning and an infrastructure of social and economic supports. The right to protection, for example, may translate well into practice when agencies, such as the police, are reliable upholders of law. When they are reliably corrupt it can be a recipe for oppression. Furthermore, some aspects of the concept of childhood contained in the UNCRC might also depend for their realization upon a level of economic wealth that many countries do not possess. As we have seen, for some countries international economic policy has led to deepening poverty, ill-health and inequality at the same time that social policy is urging the adoption of the rights of children.

Perhaps, though, this is to underestimate the subtle processes that the UNCRC is enmeshed within. The different ways in which it (or part of it, Article 12) can be interpreted illustrate well how cultural globalization creates both diversity and homogeneity. It is, as Lee (1999) has pointed out, a document that has effectivity only because it is ambiguous. It is framed in such a way that its general principles are given a great deal of space for local interpretation. In fact, such was the level of disagreement among those who drafted it that this was the only way to make it acceptable to a wide range of countries with different cultural traditions about childhood. As Lee (2001a: 95–6) comments:

> If the Convention had been intended to clarify children's position, it would indeed crumple under this burden, but the Convention operates in a rather different way. Having generated childhood ambiguity, it then lays the responsibility for managing that ambiguity on the legislatures and the policy-makers of the states that have ratified it.

The representation of childhood found in the UNCRC has become more complex and ambiguous than the earlier Declaration. The protection and provision articles of the Convention still emphasize children's need of adult support but, at the same time, especially through Article 12 of the Convention, children are pictured as social actors, not outside but inside society, not passive recipients but active participants.

Regulating children

However, the contradictory effects of globalization do not all flow in the direction of self-expression and rights. From another point of view the twentieth century has witnessed increased levels of institutional control over children. The introduction of compulsory schooling and children's formal exclusion from paid work signalled a historical tendency towards children's increasing compartmentalization in specifically designated, separate settings, supervised by professionals and structured according to age and ability. Näsman (1994) has called this process the institutionalization of childhood. Throughout the twentieth century schooling has gradually been extended both 'upwards' (for example in incremental steps towards an older leaving-age for compulsory schooling) and 'downwards' in the growing emphasis on pre-school education and nursery provision (Moss *et al.*, 2000.)

Even leisure time is often framed in this way for many children because activities such as sport or music increasingly take place within some kind of institutional setting. It can be seen in the provision of after-school and holiday clubs that organize and regulate children's activities under an adult gaze, channelling them into forms considered developmentally healthy and productive. Such phenomena have been noted across European societies. German sociologists, for example, have used the terms 'domestication' to describe the progressive removal of children from the streets and other public spaces and their relocation in special, protected spaces. They use the term 'insularization' to describe the decreased levels of children's autonomous mobility around cities and the creation of special 'islands' of childhood to and from which they are transported (Zeiher, 2001, 2002).

Within these institutions, but with significant variations according to national policy, it is possible to discern a struggle to tighten the regulation of children and to shape more firmly the outcomes of their activities. Schooling is a good example of this. In the last decades of the twentieth century the rather instrumental schooling regimes of the 'Tiger Economies' of Southeast Asia were held up as the model for producing economic efficiency and were widely influential in changing educational systems in Europe. I have argued elsewhere that this phenomenon represents a refocusing of modernity's drive to control the future through children (Prout, 2000a). This tightening of control over children derives from a declining faith in other mechanisms of economic control, combined with increasing competitive pressures from the world economy. The intensification of global competition and the intricate networking of national economies erode the state's capacity to control its own economic activity. In such circumstances, shaping children as the future labour force is seen as an increasingly important option. This, after all, is exactly what supply side economics is about but, as far as children are concerned, it often leads to attempts to regulate and standardize what they learn and how they learn it.

Conclusion

This chapter has set out the contemporary context for the study of childhood. I have suggested that childhood has been deeply implicated in, affected by and destabilized by contemporary social, technological and economic change. I started with the crisis of representation that has occurred around childhood. This both draws on and feeds back into the constitution of real childhoods, blurring the boundary between childhood and adulthood that modernity put into place. There is, I have argued, a simultaneous trend towards a common global conception of childhood but also a growing awareness of its diversity. This reflects the power of global communications to both disseminate universal conceptions and to make the local worlds of childhood more visible to each other. At the same time the diversity of childhood as a real, lived and material phenomenon is also growing. Economic globalization is changing and fragmenting the social and economic circumstances within which children grow up. These processes are creating new constructions of childhood in which children are positioned as active beings, participating in the social world. This erodes but does not completely dissolve the boundary between childhood and adulthood. The claim that childhood is disappearing is a perhaps understandable response to this situation. However, it misapprehends processes of contemporary social change because it takes for granted that childhood is a stable entity. Childhood is necessarily caught up in patterns of change because it is integral to society, history, economics – in fact to life in all its many-sided complexity.

The central theme of this book is the inadequacy of oppositional dichotomies for understanding childhood. Contemporary society, and childhood with it, is changing in ways that render these oppositions outmoded. The three aspects of the crisis of childhood representations discussed above are each characterized by such a breakdown of these oppositions. In the chapters that follow I will explore some of the emergent practices and forms that cut across these oppositions. For the moment, however, it is enough to note that the boundary between childhood and adulthood, which modernity erected and kept in place for a substantial period of time, is beginning to blur, introducing all kinds of ambiguities and uncertainties. This is the soil from which anxiety about the 'disappearance' of childhood grows and it is the feature of contemporary childhood that demands new approaches to its understanding and analysis. In particular, childhood studies should examine the processes and materials that go into the making of childhood and, in a world of change, complexity and ambiguity, should be concerned to understand what is emerging as childhood's future. However, if childhood studies are to be adequate to this task, it is necessary first to assess critically how they have approached their task in the past. In the next chapter I will, therefore, examine how childhood studies came into being, drawing out what can be learnt about the direction they need to take if they are to grapple with contemporary realities and trends.

2 Childhood studies and the modern mentality

> . . . we have to turn away from an exclusive concern with social relations and weave them into a fabric that includes non-human actants, actants that offer the possibility of holding society together as a durable whole.
>
> (Latour, 1991: 103)

Introduction

Modernity was associated not with the emergence of childhood per se but with a particular form of it that is marked by a heightened separation from adulthood. Childhood studies emerged as part of this modern concept of childhood. Belief in the separateness of childhood from adulthood was both a condition of possibility for, and an effect of, constituting childhood as a special sphere of study. The adult–child binary constituted childhood both as a distinct state of being, quite separate from adulthood, and a process of becoming adult that could be described, explored, mapped and explained. In this chapter I will trace the development of childhood studies from Darwin to the present day.

Modern childhood was brought into existence through a labour of division carried out in many different spheres. In part this was accomplished through the representation of childhood through the oppositional dualities described in Chapter 1 but it was also accomplished through material practices and the concrete organization of space in institutions such as schools and hospitals. One very important focus of this was the prolonged process by which children in Europe and the US were largely excluded from full-time paid employment but included in compulsory schooling (Cunningham, 1991; Cunningham and Viazzo, 1996; Hendrick, 1997a; Heywood, 2001; Lavalette, 1994).

This process, which took most of the nineteenth and some of the twentieth century to achieve, was a continuation of the course of events described by Aries. By the end of the nineteenth century, conceptions of children as innocent, ignorant, dependent, vulnerable, generally incompetent and in need of protection and discipline were widespread. In general terms, by the start of the twentieth these ideas had been diffused through most of the different social classes and groupings within modern society. They supported and were in turn reinforced by the effort to construct the school and the family as the 'proper place' for children. This emerged as an intended and unintended effect of many different strategies and practices. The early industrial labour movement, for example, was active in factory reform, including struggles to reduce working hours and limit child (and female) labour. One form that these campaigns took was for the family wage – that is for male workers – to be paid a level enabling them to support a non-working wife and children (Montanari, 2000). By the last part of the nineteenth century economic change, including rising standards of living, and shifts in the technology of factory production, which demanded skills at which children were not adept, also pushed in the same direction. At the same time a wide variety of social reformers worked to improve the life conditions of children, while moral reformers campaigned to 'save' children from circumstances that they believed were injurious to their souls (Pearson, 1983; Platt, 1977). These included, for example, the phenomenon found in the growing urban centres of industrialism, of households consisting entirely of children. Efforts were also made to take children away from the street and confine them to places such as the home, the school or youth organizations like the Scouts or the Boys Brigade.

The overall effect of these practices was the establishment of the idea that children do not belong in the public space. In the twentieth century this was an idea exported and disseminated through the world as part of modernization. School attendance and the removal of children from paid work became part of a universal ideal of childhood. They are today widely regarded as indices of a nation's development. They are the explicit aims of international organizations such as UNICEF and of governments, and they are seen as an essential part of the path to economic prosperity and the creation of national identity.

Through these efforts the lives of children, in the West and elsewhere, have undoubtedly been improved, sometimes dramatically so. However, the formation of modern childhood was not an unambiguously welcomed creation. For example, the historical resistance of working-class parents and children to compulsory schooling should alert us to the possibility that the measures reformers thought were good for children were not necessarily approved by everyone. This remains true today and sometimes the effort to impose the modernist ideal of childhood has quite negative results. For example, in the United States a bill was introduced in 1993 by Senator Harkin which threatened to prohibit the import into the United States of minerals obtained or manufactured goods produced with child labour. This led employers in the Bangladesh garment industry to lay off tens of thousands of mostly female child workers. A survey based on a sample of children laid off found that these had turned to other, in many cases more hazardous, activities, and that none of them had returned to school (Boyden *et al.*, 1998). This happened in part because campaigners allowed an idealized and sentimentalized idea of childhood to override better informed opinion. In particular they ignored the voices of child workers themselves, who argued against steps to expel them from work, insisting that what they wanted was to combine work with education. They understood that their work made an essential contribution to their families and communities and that without it their situation would only worsen.

This example underlines how the exclusion of children from the public sphere, on the assumption that they are too ignorant to have an opinion of any worth or that their interests are best articulated by adults, can have very problematic consequences. The same issue also stands behind the widespread sexual abuse of children in the care of the state (Kendrick, 1998). It is part, too, of the story of the cruelty and neglect which occurred when British children, in the care of Barnardos, were involuntarily sent to Australia (Buti, 2002). Being placed under the master identity of ideal childhood involved dependence and exclusion from the public world and this could have a high cost.

In fact, however, the separation of childhood from adulthood has never been completely achieved anywhere. There were many sources of resistance. As noted above, in nineteenth-century Europe many working-class parents resisted the idea that their children should be at school rather than earning income to contribute to the household budget. Children's school attendance was ensured by a mixture of enforcement, through the efforts of school attendance officers and the courts, and of persuasion to the view that school is the best and most appropriate place for their long-term development. Today, in many parts of the world, the modern ideal simply cannot, for economic or social reasons, be achieved – even if there is cultural and political agreement with it.

However, as suggested in Chapter 1, alongside the global diffusion of the modern ideal of childhood, there are also signs that the boundary between children and adults is blurring and becoming destabilized. In the face of this there are many efforts to maintain and renew children's separation from adults by ensuring that they are kept in their proper places. Education systems around the world show a trend to more and more instrumental testing and the heightened surveillance of children (Goldstein and Heath, 2000). As schools struggle with the widespread disaffection of children, 'truancy' has re-emerged as a topic of social policy. New and tougher measures to compel and persuade recalcitrant children and parents to school attendance are being invented (Social Exclusion Unit, 1998). In South America street children who, for whatever reason, have become detached from their kinship network are subject to vicious prejudice and semi-official murder campaigns to sweep them away (Scheper-Hughes and Hoffman, 1988). In the UK and the US there has been an upsurge in the recourse to youth and child curfews as a weapon to remove them from public space (Hemmens and Bennett, 1999).

The modern mentality

The creation of childhood in its modern form was the historical background against which childhood studies emerged. The practices that constituted modernity also shaped childhood studies and their genealogy is imbricated with them. In order to illuminate this relationship further it is necessary, first, to re-open the question of how to characterize modernity, extending the discussion started in Chapter 1. In fact it is necessary to question what almost all accounts of modernity take for granted – the claim that it is in some fundamental way a break with all that went before. This assumption largely mirrors the belief that modern people have about themselves and it is one that even social critics share. Marx and Engels (1848/1968), for example, in a famous passage written in 1848 extol the revolutionary power of capitalism in a way that expresses this view:

> The bourgeoisie cannot exist without constantly revolutionizing the instruments of production, and thereby the relations of production, and with them the whole relations of society . . . Constant revolutionizing of production, uninterrupted disturbance of all social conditions, ever-lasting uncertainty and agitation distinguish the bourgeois epoch from all earlier ones. All fixed, fast-frozen relations, with their train of ancient and venerable prejudices and opinions, are swept away, all new formed ones become antiquated before they can ossify. All that is solid melts into air, all that is holy is profaned.

This is a powerful passage, epic in its tone and prescient about the rapidity of social change that characterizes our own time as well as theirs. But should we believe everything about the story they tell? At the simplest level we can ask whether there were not also continuities with the past. Was not modernity made from the same materials as pre-modernity? Or at least the same sort of materials even if they were combined and elaborated in new kinds of ways? After all, few would argue that modernity came into being through a 'big bang'. Its cultural, political, technological and economic aspects developed unevenly and with different genealogies, such that modernity's periodization is problematic. There were continuities as well as ruptures in the process. When we are ourselves caught up in the very processes that we wish to understand, when we can be considered products of them, it is easy to exaggerate our difference with other phases of human existence. This is especially so when we have a stake in the claim of novelty and, often implicit in it, of the superiority of modernity over other forms of society.

So how are we to understand modernity without assuming its own self-proclaimed novelty or superiority? How can we hold these questions open? The approach that I advocate in this book starts with the idea that society, including childhood, is a heterogeneous assembly. What is called modernity emerged through a multitude of different materials, ideas and practices. Some of these were material – the inventions implicated in the Industrial Revolution, or buildings such as the hospital, the school, the prison and the barrack. Some of these were representational – they were ways of looking at and categorizing the world. They were discursive, linguistic and symbolic. However, even this distinction between the material and the representational is, from the point of view of heterogeneity, quite inadequate. Most of the entities that populate modernity are products of *both* material and representational processes and one would be hard-pressed indeed to separate these different components from each other.

However, for the moment, before returning to issues of the interconnection of the representational and the material, I want to dwell on the modes of thought and representation that are associated with modernity. According to Bauman the basic project of modernity was the search for order, purity and the drive to exclude ambivalence. As a consequence he writes:

> The horror of mixing reflects the obsession with separating . . . The central frame of both modern intellect and modern practice is opposition – more precisely, dichotomy.
>
> (Bauman, 1991: 14)

Modernist thinking is marked by the proliferation of such dichotomies. The division between childhood and adulthood, and their association with various qualities that I discussed in Chapter 1, is an example of this. It is also well illustrated by modernist social theory, which proceeds by dividing the social world into discrete aspects each set in relation to its opposite: structure versus agency; local versus global; identity versus difference; continuity versus change . . . and so on. A particular dualism, that of nature and culture, is, however, not only a very important axis of modernist thinking but has, I want to suggest, a particular salience to the trajectory taken by childhood studies during the modern period.

Culture and nature

It is widely agreed that the culture–nature binary, that is the division of the world into two mutually exclusive kinds of entity, is a feature of post-Enlightenment thinking. The broad effect of this was to challenge the view of society and nature promulgated in religious belief, more specifically that of the Catholic Church. The central element of this challenge was a belief in natural science as a model for the development of human understanding (and control). The blend of rationalism and empiricism that underlay this idea of science made great claim to the idea of universal knowledge. Science could be applied everywhere with the expectation that it would produce knowledge that would be true everywhere, irrespective of the cultural context.

Latour (1993) addresses modernity from this perspective in his book *We Have Never Been Modern*. He sees the emergence of the nature–culture divide as a product of this claim to universal knowledge and discusses this through an instance of its inauguration. This instance is the real but largely overlooked debate between Boyle, the seventeenth-century scientist and inventor of the air-pump, and the philosopher Thomas Hobbes (see Schapin and Scheffer, 1985). The nub of their debate revolved around the legitimacy of gatherings of independently minded citizens coming to conclusions about facts, in other words creating knowledge. For Boyle, the empirical scientist, laboratory practice consisted of not only building machines (of which his air-pump is a celebrated example) with which to experimentally test competing theories of nature, it also involved a specific kind of dramatic social gathering: the experiment as a public event. In the experiment respectable men of good character observed the public demonstration of a claim to knowledge or proof. In this public setting they could attest to or contest the veracity of the experimental procedures and the facticity of their results. To Hobbes, the monarchist philosopher, this conception of the experiment as a public event was anathema. The modern state, he argued, was only possible if citizens accepted that a central power, constitutional monarchy, spoke with authority. The voice of the monarch was the voice of all the citizens speaking as they would speak were they able to speak together. In the Hobbesian view, knowledge and power are inseparable. The notion that groups of citizens should speak of truth independently could not be tolerated and Hobbes consequently opposed Boyle's empirical, experimental theatre of science as an unconstitutional and subversive source of knowledge.

So far one might view this story as one of enlightenment versus prejudice. But Latour's crucial point is that Boyle and Hobbes reached a settlement of their argument. Hobbes was able to accept the possibility of empirical science so long as its object, nature, was thought of as distinct and separate from society and was to be spoken for by scientists. In mirror-image fashion, Boyle could be content with the assigning of nature to a science which was constituted as uncontaminated by the contingencies of society, culture and politics. The official, visible discourse of modernity was constituted on this dualism and it became an episteme of subsequent Western discourse. The essence of his argument is that what has been called modernism consists of a double set of practices. On the one hand, the spheres of nature and culture have been kept separate, with nature assigned to 'science', thought of as a culture-free, socially neutral practice that produces truth. On the other hand, modernity also produced a submerged, unacknowledged but crucial proliferation of entities which are hybrids of culture and nature. These are the technologies, devices, machines, techniques and knowledges of modernity – the very basis of its claim to a basic difference from pre-modern societies. They are hybrids of culture and nature because they depend upon natural phenomena (chemical reactions, interactions between forces, the collision of electrons, etc.) but they are not of nature. Without the social and cultural institutions of science, technology, economy, education, politics and so on they would not exist. These technologies, therefore, constitute the stuff of modern societies but at the same time their hybrid character is occluded and denied by modernity's separation of culture and nature.

Purification and mediation

This double move to separate nature and culture and, covertly, hybridize them requires two different kinds of intellectual work. On the one hand, there is the *work of mediation*, taking place in the laboratories and workshops of modern society and through which hybrid entities of culture–nature (like the PC on which I am producing this text) are fabricated. On the other, there is the *work of purification*, the practices by which distinctions between the world of nature and the world of culture and society are created and maintained. Modernist discourse is thus constructed as a set of extremely powerful interlocking concepts which until recently have proved difficult to crack open. Latour argues that this mentality is able to hold together a series of paradoxical images:

- Nature is transcendent and humans can do nothing against its laws.
- Nature is immanent in the practices of science and gives humans unlimited possibilities.
- Society is immanent and humans are free to construct it as we wish.
- Society is transcendent and humans can do nothing against its laws.

Seen in these terms modernist thinking seems to block all the escape routes and cover all possibilities. But in Latour's account something else is also happening. While modernism separates nature and culture it simultaneously proliferates hybrids. Every device, machine, technology is neither pure nature nor pure culture but a networked set of associations, which deny the purity of either. They are hybrid socio-technical networks. The scale of this proliferation has now become so great that the modernist edifice has become insupportable. One obvious example of this is the environmental crisis brought sharply to our attention by Green social activists around the world and now widely recognized as a serious problem. This arises because the translated products of nature that we call technology cannot be separated from nature itself. Every CFC aerosol contributes to the hole in the ozone layer, every internal combustion engine adds to the greenhouse effect, and every factory trawler contributes to the declining stocks of fish. Another startling example, which I will return to in Chapter 5, is the human genome project, in which nature and culture are utterly imbricated.

Of course Latour is not the only theorist to notice these tendencies. In her famous essay *A Cyborg Manifesto*, Haraway (1991) urges the importance of the 'cyborg image' for understanding feminist politics in an age when the human and the technical are conspicuously merging. We cannot, she argues, understand modern societies except by understanding the ways in which we, as humans, are produced within and are inseparable from socio-technical and biological networks. At the same time Marilyn Strathern (1991), in her ethnographic work on Melanesia, reminds us that the separation of nature and culture is not a universal feature of human thought. Discussing Melanesian artefacts such as the ritual in which a spirit face moves up and down a column, she describes it as a Melanesian cyborg. But, she points out:

> The distinction between the Melanesian cyborg and Haraway's half human, half mechanical contraption is that the components of the Melanesian cyborg are 'cut' from the same material. There is no difference between shell strands and a matrilineage, between a man and a bamboo pole, between a yam and a spirit.
>
> (Strathern, 1991: 118)

From this point of view, however, the boundary between the modern and the pre-modern becomes much less clear than modernist thought wishes to allow. Pre-modernity and modernity share their hybridization of nature and culture. Modernity's distinction is that it denies that it also combines and connects nature and culture through the work of science and technology. It devotes, at least until recently, gigantic intellectual efforts to the work of purification.

Indeed, according to Latour, a general shape to these efforts can be discerned. This traces the separation of culture and nature from its formal codification by Kant through to the despairing, nihilistic, suicidal pre-occupations of postmodernists with their hyper-realities, free-floating signifiers and deep, impenetrable, ineffable, decentred but pathological communicative codes. The general pattern of modernist thought is that the separation of nature and culture is progressively widened by the construction of categories of thought that attempt to keep nature and culture each in their place. The dualism is codified, for example, in Kant's formal distinction between the objects (of nature) and the subjects (of human culture). The distance between them is extended by Hegelian notions of contradiction. It is widened again in the phenomenological idea of an insurmountable tension between subject and object. The divide is pushed still wider by Habermas's declaration that in the modern world the main danger to free-speaking human subjects comes from the objects produced through rational–instrumental science and technology. This attempt to retain the distinction between culture and nature reaches its absurd zenith in the more or less complete separation of (cultural) human subjects and the material conditions of life in postmodernism. The archetype is Baudrillard's infamous contention that the Gulf War never occurred except as a hyper-real illusion of TV.

At this point in the trajectory of modernist thought, sometimes called postmodernism, it is apparent that the culture side of the nature–culture duality (symbols, representations, discourse, subjectivity) has achieved (or is declared to have achieved) a kind of semiotic autonomy. All relationship between the world of culture and that of nature is abandoned. All the intricate networking of symbols and material, and of human and non-human entities, that concretely constitutes the accomplishment of modern practice is simply bracketed out. There is declared to be no relationship between culture and nature, nothing is seen to mediate or connect them. The social and cultural are treated as if they were autonomous realms.

In the face of these ever more desperate efforts to keep nature and culture apart Latour poses a stark and radical alternative. We should, he argues, stop moving on in this ever more absurd direction. We should retrace our steps so that modern 'natures–cultures' become the topic of our investigation. If this were done then, he argues, it would be possible to understand how modernity separated culture and nature while at the same time intensively hybridizing them. Culture and nature, objects and subjects, human and non-human, representations and referents and so on would appear not as different species of being but as complex combinations. The natures–cultures of modernity could be apprehended on much the same terms that anthropologists have understood them in pre-modern societies. Like the pre-moderns the moderns also mix up nature and culture. The key difference is that the moderns have consistently denied that they do any such thing. It is, however, only when we pay attention to *both* the work of mediating (associating, networking) nature and culture *and* purifying (disassociating, separating) that the distance between pre-modern and modern societies shrinks to the point that the anthropological habit of speaking in the same breath about people, things, animals, environments, bodies, theories, beliefs, spirits becomes possible in relation to modern societies. This means that 'we have never been modern', in the sense that modernity can no longer be regarded as a radical break with all previous human societies.

History of childhood studies

At this point the reader may be wondering what on earth any of this has to do with childhood studies. There seems to be a long distance between these rather abstract discussions and studying childhood – and an even greater one between them and the practical business of being a child. But in fact the distance is a rather short one. This becomes clearer if we ask a fundamental question: 'What is a child?'. In fact modernity has had a great deal of trouble answering this question. As Haraway's (1991) argument implies children are one of those categories that elude the nature–culture dichotomy that (at one level) modernity erected. They seem to hang somewhere between the two. I will argue in the rest of this book that the future of childhood studies rests on finding ways of treating childhood as a 'nature–culture'. Thus I want to argue that only by understanding the ways in which childhood is constructed by the heterogeneous elements of culture and nature, which in any case cannot be easily separated, will it be possible to take the field forward. Latour uses the phrase 'the heterogeneous networks of the social' to capture the idea that human society is created through a complex set of mediations between culture and nature. In a striking phrase he says that these networks are:

> simultaneously real, like nature, narrated, like discourse and collective, like society.

(Latour, 1993: 6)

I think this is a truly fitting apothegm for childhood studies and I will return to it in later chapters. However, for the moment I will examine how childhood studies have handled the nature–culture relationship. I will argue that the history of childhood studies describes a trajectory through this relationship, which, because it has operated within a modernist field of thought that separated culture and nature, zig-zags between the poles of the opposition, now placing childhood at the biological end, now at the social. Sometimes it has found a more or less uneasy compromise that included both but this has proved hard to stabilize because it is constantly undercut by definitions of nature and culture that are mutually exclusive. When it explored childhood from the biological point of view it discovered that it could not be contained within a pure realm of nature. In fact, as I will show, through biology it came to the social. In more recent times, however, it has turned to a purely social view of childhood but it has done this in a way that separates biology from culture, bracketing it off or even denying it.

Darwin and the Child Study movement

It is often claimed that the beginnings of modern childhood studies can be found in the work of Charles Darwin. While it is true that Darwin became fascinated with children's development, and substantially contributed to its understanding, his claim to be the origin of this interest is contestable. For example, Darwin's own grandfather had published on the topic, the German philosopher Tiedeman wrote about it in 1787 (Denis, 1972) and, as Steadman (1982) reports, the archives of many regional libraries in the UK are full of unpublished observational notes written by mothers about their children. It seems wiser to assume that children and their ways have been of perpetual interest to curious adults from time immemorial.

However, in some important sense Darwin does represent an important beginning for the history of modern studies of childhood. It was through his interest that, in the nineteenth and early twentieth centuries, the subject became saturated with notions of biological universality. In fact, however, Darwin himself may not have intended this inflection to be quite as strong as it came to be. He kept observational notes of his first child, William, who was born in 1839, eight years after he set out on his famous voyage on the good ship *Beagle*, during which he formed his key ideas about the theory of evolution. These notes on William are copious and wide-ranging, containing many interesting speculations, for example on what appears to be instinctive and what appears to be learnt. Darwin used these observations in two later books, *The Expression of Emotions in Man and Animals*, published in 1872, and *Biographical Sketch of an Infant*, published in 1877. One of his main arguments in these texts is that human children quickly acquire the capacity to understand their caretakers. This happens before they have the capacity to understand language. Children's capacity to derive meaning from what is being communicated by their caretakers seems to be accomplished by reading the expression on their faces and the intonation of their words. Darwin took this to be an indication that human capacities have evolved gradually from those exercised by our animal ancestors. It is interesting, however, that what he took to use in his writing is just a small selection from his earlier notes. His overall aim was to highlight the role of biological processes in human development. This is understandable given the furore that his ideas on evolution had created amongst the religious establishment but it, nevertheless, meant that his focus became relatively narrow when compared to the broad-ranging and humanistic observations of his notebooks. For example, he pays relatively little attention to higher mental processes, a fact that mirrors his public confession (sincere or otherwise) that he felt he had little aptitude for such work.

Nevertheless, Darwin's writings triggered a wave of interest in child development in the form of the Child Study movement. The heyday of this activity lasted from the 1880s through to the second decade of the twentieth century, though its influence lasted much longer than this. Its approach can be characterized in two ways. First, it claimed the status of science. As James Sully (quoted in Woodhead, 2003) wrote in 1895:

> Ours is a scientific age, and science has cast its inquisitive eye on the infant . . . we now speak of the beginning of careful and methodical investigation of child nature, by men trained in scientific observation.

The lure of science for nineteenth-century thinkers cannot be underestimated. Conservatives and revolutionaries alike sought to claim its kudos. What they claimed to base their thinking on was, however, a thoroughly nineteenth-century notion of science. Science, they believed, meant the discovery and statement of universal laws, uncovered through the devising of theories, from which predictions could be derived and tested by observation and experiment. Much (but not all) of twentieth-century developmental psychology is rooted in this approach. Although this vision of science continues to have a powerful position, the twentieth century has also seen the emergence of new approaches to science that do not make the same claims. Indeed, as I shall argue in later chapters, current understanding of many natural and social phenomena is that they are complex and non-linear in character – and hence not comprehensible through the apparatus of deterministic prediction.

However, in large measure the Darwinian legacy tied childhood studies in their earliest phase to a largely biological view of childhood. Hendrick (1997b: 48) sums up the situation thus:

> In effect, Child Study helped to spread the techniques of natural history to the study of children, showing them to be 'natural creatures'; through its lectures, literature and the practice of its influential members, it popularised the view that the child's conception differed from that of adults, that there were marked stages in normal mental development; and that there were similarities between the mental worlds of children and primitives.

As this quote hints, the reasons for the popularity of this approach are not accounted for solely by the intellectual force of the argument or by Darwin's status as a giant of scientific thinking. Viewing the child as a natural primitive also played into nineteenth- and twentieth-century concerns with empire and race. The child became an instance of the Other, a homologue for all such 'primitives' and a demonstration of the gulf that divided the 'civilized' from the 'uncivilized'. This divide was applied both to internal social divisions, such as the abiding concern of nineteenth- and twentieth-century social policy with how to handle the 'troublesome classes', and to external Others like the subjects of imperial rule, deemed racially inferior. However, alongside its ideological kinship with such ideas, the Child Study movement can also be seen as part of another key development of the nineteenth century – the construction of children as a concern of the Nation. The advent of compulsory schooling in the industrializing societies of Europe and North America gave children as a social group an unprecedented visibility. Much 'biopolitical' concern, to use Foucault's term, was generated through research and discussion about the physical and mental state of what came to be seen as a national resource for international military and economic competition. Children became a target for investment and were seen as the 'children of the nation' (Hendrick, 1997b: 49).

The Child Study movement per se was in decline by the first decade of the twentieth century. Although its lasting legacy, which did not begin to be seriously questioned in mainstream childhood studies until the latter half of the twentieth century, was its emphasis on the biological roots of behaviour and its preference for an (albeit nineteenth-century) idea of scientific knowledge. Paradoxically, however, despite its roots in a biological conception of the child, it helped to create a situation in which childhood was no longer seen to occur naturally. It did this by promoting the idea that childhood needed the attention and intervention of experts. The opening of this space accounts for many of the developments in the study of children in the decades up to and beyond the Second World War. What started as an essentially biological project, locating childhood as a natural phenomenon, saw a growing awareness of the social ramifications of childhood. Childhood studies thus described an uneven trajectory during which they gradually accreted these social elements.

Paediatric medicine

One of the disciplines contributing to childhood studies that witnessed such an accretion of the 'social' to the 'biological' was the emerging science of paediatric medicine. In tracing this process Armstrong (1983) argues that from the end of the eighteenth century the representations of the body found in medical atlases were constructed through new forms of disciplinary power, those which Foucault famously termed 'panoptical' and which were associated with new techniques of surveillance. These centred on the processes of clinical observation in the hospital (to which the sick, especially the poor sick, were taken from their homes) and of the anatomy bench (through which the inner workings of the body were made visible). The sick person and their body thus came under the intense, microscopic, scrutinizing gaze of the doctor, and his or her symptoms were recorded, described and classified. As specific conditions were localized to particular locations in the body, an anatomical atlas and pathology were summoned into existence. However, although these observations and measurements were repeated millions of times, the body that was constructed through them was an individual, biological one. It remained so because its trace and repository was the individual case note. This was, as yet, a body without the means to project itself into the social.

   What changed this was the development, towards the end of the nineteenth century, of the institution of the dispensary. In the Edinburgh dispensary described by Armstrong, the main work was to treat tubercolic patients at an outpatient clinic and to arrange home visits to sufferers whose needs could be assessed and living conditions discovered. This migration from and extension of the clinic to the community setting created an enormous new terrain for panoptical practices:

   The Dispensary further refined this [medical] gaze, these techniques of analysis, to fix them, not on individual bodies so much as the interstices of society; [it] was a mechanism of power which imposed on the

spatial arrangements of bodies the social configuration of their relationship . . . a device, above all else, for making visible to constant
surveillance the interaction between people, normal and abnormal, and
thereby transforming the physical space between bodies into social space
traversed by power. At the beginning of the twentieth century the
'social' was born as an autonomous realm.

(Armstrong, 1983: 9–10)

Armstrong is, of course, not the first to borrow and develop this account
of the emergence of disciplinary society from Foucault. Donzelot (1979)
makes essentially the same point in relation to the surveillance of the family
in France. As he points out, children were the points of access for the surveillance of the French family, the great moral cause that sanctioned the
breaching of its privacy. In the US, too, child saving was an influential and
important social movement (Platt, 1977).

Children were also enmeshed in other panoptical powers, exercised
through mass schooling, which overlapped with the medical ones. The
understanding of childhood disease as a specific and separate branch of
medicine emerged alongside the extension of the modern ideal of childhood to greater and greater numbers of children from wider and wider
social classes. Through the intersection of educational and medical regimes
childhood became one of the main targets for new practices of pre-
ventive medicine, applied, for instance, through milk depots at which
bottled milk was provided to mothers with small babies. At each weekly
attendance the child was weighed, and their homes were visited by health
visitors who kept records on their progress. This surveillance was extended
in 1908 when regular health inspection of children in school began.
The Society for the Study of Diseases of Children was founded in 1901
and the British Paediatric Society in 1928. By the first quarter of the
twentieth century, then, mechanisms were in place in the UK, and
with parallels in other countries, through which the health of children
could become a topic in its own right and be measured and monitored in
systematic ways.

However, it was not until the Second World War that paediatrics found
a panoptical device through which the social aspect of childhood was
brought into full refinement. This device was the child health survey.
In the UK, survey techniques can be traced back to the nineteenth century,
where the work of the Rowntrees and Booth springs immediately to mind,
and in the medical sphere were developed in the inter-war period. Studies
of child development had been carried out in the US by Gesell during
the 1920s, although these were still relatively small samples and often carried
out in special observation domes rather than in the settings and communities in which the children lived. Nevertheless, the survey's high-water
mark in the UK was in the post-1945 era with the institution of the longitudinal survey. Four main English surveys started, respectively, in 1946,

1958, 1970 and 2000. These studies continue to track cohorts of children and their descendants. The 1958 study, for example, is currently tracking the grandchildren of those born at the start of the study. These longitudinal studies had their counterparts in countries around the world and were added to by many cross-sectional studies looking at different aspects of child growth, development and rearing. During the second half of the twentieth century a vast amount of data on many of the key physical, behavioural and emotional patterns of growth were established, at least for children growing up in the industrialized countries. Normal development and growth, the product of hundreds of thousands of individual measurements, was used as the template against which the abnormal could be identified.

In such studies the development and growth of nationally representative samples of children could be tracked over time. Through this the object that was constructed was not the pathology of the individual child, as had proliferated in the pre-war period, but a picture of the 'normal child'. It was this emphasis on the normal, together with the developmental perspective, that gave paediatrics its distinction as a medical speciality. Through this it was possible to draw together under the umbrella of paediatrics 'such diverse aspects of growth as the biochemical and immunological, the intellectual, the emotional and the social' (Apley, cited in Armstrong, 1983: 59).

This broad multi-dimensional perspective could be readily endorsed by social scientists. For example, in their book *Sociology in Medicine*, devoted to showing that social factors are an important component of understanding disease, Susser and Watson (1962), respectively Senior Lecturers in Social Medicine and Social Anthropology at Manchester University, drew together these perspectives, stating that:

> Children in all societies pass through three main stages in the process of social maturation. These stages correspond with major changes in physical and mental growth. The first stage is that of social infancy, from birth to about the age of seven; the second is childhood, from seven to the onset of puberty; and the third is adolescence, from puberty to social acceptance as an adult. The duration of each stage, as well as the behaviour considered appropriate to it, differs from one society to another, partly because diet and habitat influence rates of physical development, and partly because the behaviour that is expected from a child in each stage is socially determined. The behaviour of children in each stage is therefore an outcome of the interplay of physiological, social and cultural forces.

Such a statement describes the arc from the biological to the social, which paediatrics as a form of child study had travelled over the previous period. It arrived at a place where the biological and the social could be added together. They could coexist so long as neither category was examined too closely. However, such a state of affairs was, as we will see, rather unstable.

Child psychology

The second emerging discipline of the twentieth century, and the one that perhaps most directly took on the mantle of the Child Study movement, was child psychology. The history of child psychology in the twentieth century is a highly complex matter, which it is only possible to summarize briefly in the space available here. In the first place it overlaps with the developments in paediatrics described above. In 1944, for example, the British Paediatric Association created a Child Psychology Sub-Committee concerned to challenge too firm a line between physical and psychological disabilities. Illingworth's (1986) landmark paediatric text, *The Normal Child*, was as concerned with psychological development as it was with physical and these concerns were both rolled up into the wave of surveys that aimed to establish patterns of growth and their correlates.

Child psychology has developed a large number of different theoretical schools and strands. One was based on the stimulus–response theories of learning associated with the behaviourism of Skinner. Another strand is found in the various schools of psychoanalysis that grew from Freud's work, dealing with instinct, early childhood experiences, and latterly the emotional complexity of language. A further area of interest is in how children acquire language: by imitation or because their brains are pre-programmed with formal grammatical structures and primed to generate speech? Yet another strand, attachment theory, is concerned with early emotional life and the mother–child tie. Perhaps most influential of all, was the work of Piaget on the development of cognitive ability, especially the powers of formal reasoning.

Whatever its particular approach, psychology remains, even in the present time, the dominant academic discipline concerned with childhood. Its concern with the individual child won an almost hegemonic position among the emerging social sciences of the early twentieth century. As Rose (1989) has suggested, its wide range of topics and approaches to children, which he terms the 'psy complex', became closely entwined with the emergence of health and welfare policies and practices around children. These too were, according to Rose, a form of biopolitics through which the state and others sought to define and regulate normality. Psychologists set about examining and testing children in order to define the 'normal' range of functioning and behaviour. In the process they constituted what was abnormal, pathological and in need of intervention. These processes straddled the main locales of children's lives but were especially concentrated in nurseries and schools. Their object of intervention was often the family and, as many have noted, the child became the entry point for the state and other agencies into the family. From the 1920s onwards, and up to the present day, there was a proliferation of professions concerned with identifying children's abnormality and attending in some way to it: child guidance clinics, educational psychology services, school attendance officers and so on. These practices have, in turn, demonstrated a huge appetite for child study, represented in the libraries of books and papers, and the dozens of professional associations and research institutes that are its inheritance.

Such psychological discourses of the child became part of a more general public consciousness. By the mid-twentieth century popularizing texts from Truby King to Benjamin Spock reflected the latest psychological thinking about what children need for their proper upbringing. Through these the language of child psychology entered everyday talk and practice. Terms like 'potty training', 'stage of development', 'bonding' and so on became the everyday stuff of childcare. Experts were on hand to advise parents, dispensing their counsel in a huge range of magazines and TV programmes, cementing psychology into place as the 'natural' place for childhood to be located as an object of knowledge.

However, towards the end of the twentieth century there was growing criticism of how psychology handled childhood. This came from both within and outside psychology as a discipline. Rather than seeing childhood as a universal constant, whether biological or cultural, in the post-Aries intellectual landscape it became possible to think of childhood as a variable and changing entity. This insight was greatly strengthened by the findings of social and cultural anthropology, which reinforced this possibility. Psychology was not immune from these arguments and they marked its discussions in many ways. By the 1970s a critical psychology began to emerge that was much more sensitive to the social context of behaviour. Significant and influential statements of this new thinking in psychology were, for example, found in volumes edited by Richards (1974) and Richards and Light (1986). In their second collection (Richards and Light, 1986: 3) they commented:

> A central theme in the earlier volume was the criticism of a psychology based on universal laws that were supposed to hold good across all societies and at all historical times. It was argued that terms such as 'the mother' and 'the child' not only conveyed a meaningless generality but misrepresented the relationship between individuals and social worlds and portrayed social arrangements as if they were fixed laws of nature.

Arguably, in some European traditions social context had not been so pushed to the margins as it had been in the Anglo-US tradition. Be that as it may, critical perspectives, although they had by no means won a majority by the 1980s, were on the ascendant. At the centre of this critical approach was the notion that children are shaped by their different social contexts and that this cannot be left out of the psychological account.

One such influential statement of this came from Bronfenbrenner (1979). The so-called 'ecological model' of development describes multiple societal systems that, when visually depicted, are represented as concentric circles. The innermost circle of the ecological environment is referred to as the microsystem and represents the most direct day-to-day reality for children and families, such as their home, school or neighbourhood settings. Individuals within the system are viewed as dynamic and continually in development. Linkages or interrelationships between settings (i.e. home, school, workplace, neighbourhood) are called mesosystems. In a separate circle, exosystems refer to one or more settings that do not directly involve, but do affect persons. Examples include a parent's workplace and its indirect effect on a child, or a community network of friends who support one another. The outermost circle or system is referred to as the macrosystem. The macrosystem represents broad interconnected beliefs, attitudes and social systems such as economics, media, immigration or public policy decisions. The social–ecological approach makes the assumption that development is a reciprocal process of interaction and accommodation across the life cycle involving the individual in increasingly large contexts. Although depicted as separate circles, users of this approach are urged to think of it as entailing reciprocity and interaction between individuals and their multiple environments.

Even more radical was the approach of the Russian psychologist L.S. Vygotsky (1962, 1978), whose ideas, developed in the Soviet Union during the 1920s, were increasingly taken up by Western psychologists from the 1960s onwards. Basing his ideas within Marxist conceptions of dialectical materialism, Vygotsky emphasized the role of social and cultural life in children's cognitive development. Underlying his approach was a concern to develop a psychology that could encompass both social and biological concerns. At this time psychology was divided between those who saw a separate and independent entity, human consciousness, as the object of their study and those who saw psychological processes as an epiphenomenon of biology and physiology. Vygotsky attempted to transcend this dualism through the notion of *mediated action*. The notion here is that during socialization children internalize the means of being part of a culture through their participation in common activities with other human beings. The elements that they acquire as a part of this process include language, beliefs, norms, facts, artefacts and modes of acting. According to Vygotsky, society provides the symbolic tools, both material and linguistic, which shape the development of thinking. Cognition can, thus, not be separated from the conditions and practices of life with which a child grows up. Indeed, thinking is not seen as located in the head of an individual but in the interaction, that is the material activity, that takes place between the individual and the collectively constituted and historically situated culture created through joint activity.

The rise of the social

By the 1980s it was clear that childhood studies, through their engagement with children as biological entities, had been brought, in both paediatrics and psychology, to a position where the importance of society and culture was fully recognized. This is not to say that the way in which the social was incorporated into thinking was in any way adequate. In the first place, social life was usually imported into medical and psychological thinking under the rubric of the same scientific method, with its claim to the objective and value-free production of facts, that was used to deal with biological phenomena. Although the outer reaches of these disciplines may have started to question the universal applicability of science, in general terms social life was admitted to knowledge on the same terms as nature. Second, the accretion of the social aspect to thinking about childhood did not happen uniformly. The process was more akin to a genealogy in which certain branches or practitioners of the disciplines concerned were able to create new, more socially aware versions of their craft while leaving other streams of thinking more or less untouched. The picture was one in which the addition of the social to the biological and psychological formed a mosaic. Here there was a lively acceptance of the social aspect, there it remained unconsidered. This is, of course, the normal state of affairs in intellectual development.

Perhaps the underlying reason for this picture is that in general (apart from pioneers such as Vygotsky, who was only just becoming recognized in Western thinking) the methodology was generally additive. Modernist modes of thought meant that nature and culture were thought of as two more or less equivalent but different principles. The key questions were about 'how much' of each could be seen as constituting the mix. Implicit in this additive approach was a dualistic assumption about nature and culture. This is well-captured by Cole's (1998) discussion of the three dualistic models of nature and culture that he sees as dominating theory about children's development in the twentieth century. Each sees an interaction between biology and culture. The first is represented by Gesell who recognizes both biology and culture as important but places most weight on endogenous processes of biological growth. In this view, while the social environment can affect the intensity and timing of development it cannot influence its basic direction, because this is determined by inherent, maturational mechanisms. The basic picture is the same in the second stream of psychological thought, behaviourism, except that in this case the estimate of quantity is reversed. The biological material is likened to an inert lump of clay, which is shaped and sculpted by the action of operant conditioning, whose source is the social environment. The third, represented by Piaget, is a somewhat more sophisticated but still dualistic account. Here equal weight is given to biological and social environmental factors, which are pictured as interacting together. However, Piaget is adamant that individuals are also an active factor shaping their developmental pathway because they are involved in making adaptations to their environment.

Social constructionism

Inadequate though these dualistic formulations were they each had the merit of viewing the child as heterogeneous, as somehow both biological and social. This position was to be radically disturbed in the final decades of the twentieth century. The first source of this was the politicization of the nature–culture debate that took place in the 1970s and 1980s around the sociobiology episode. I will discuss this at greater length in Chapter 4. At this point, however, it can simply be noted that the first wave of sociobiological ideas repelled most social scientists by its tendency towards the reduction of social life to biological precepts. Furthermore, the 'social' and 'biological' sides of this debate became politicized, so that advocates of sociobiology were associated with right-wing ideas and its opponents with left-wing ones. This polarized the debate creating a climate within which it was difficult to explore what the connections between biology and culture might be.

The second source of ideas that undermined the exploration of the heterogeneous materials from which social life is constructed was also in part a reaction to the reductionism of the sociobiologists. This was the appearance of an influential set of ideas that came to be known as 'social constructionism'. In its most general sense this term refers to what is almost axiomatic in the sociological tradition: that reality is made in specific social circumstances and varies across both history and culture, and is open to change both intended and unintended. This position is also dualistic about nature and culture. The effect of social constructionism is to separate out what is 'social' from what is 'biological', in order to create the terrain on which social analysis can take place. The tendency is to make the territory of the social as large as possible by winning as much from biology as possible, conceding to it, if at all possible, only a residue. For instance, to take an example not directly related to childhood, when it comes to sex, the social constructionist position is to draw a boundary between 'sex' (usually a residual area conceded to biology) while claiming all the most important phenomena as part of 'gender', that is to say historical and cultural phenomena. This has led later feminist critics, such as Haraway (1991: 134), to argue that contemporary feminism must be consistent in its rejection of the binary logics of the nature/culture pair by extending it to the sex/gender distinction.

However, the social constructionist position, as it was developed towards the end of the twentieth century, went a good deal further than simply opposing nature to culture. This occurred as it came under the influence of that combination of sociological hermeneutics and post-structuralist linguistics that is known as the 'linguistic turn' in social theory. Since Weber, sociologists have argued that, because social action and interaction are meaningful, social life has hermeneutic properties. It can and, in a sense, must be interpreted or read like a text. Structural and post-structuralist linguistic theory was most strongly developed first in literary studies and then in a web of ideas that informed the emergence of cultural studies. However, these ideas have been influential throughout the social sciences. Most importantly the linguistic turn pressed the idea that society is constructed through language and in this sense can not only be treated as a text but *is* a text. In (post)structuralist thinking texts are entities unto themselves. Meaning is not generated by referents outside the texts but by the structure of relationships between the terms of the text. The great strength of this position is that it supports a view of language that accords it power to create and not just simply reflect its referents. The more the nuts and bolts of making a representation are made visible, the more it becomes apparent that what is produced is not a stable, fixed mirror image of the 'reality' that is being represented. Representations cannot be taken at face value. Different representations of the 'same' thing can be produced, reflecting different points of view and social interests.

However, the problem with this linguistic turn is, as Latour (1993: 63–4) puts it, that it:

> [renders] more difficult the connections between an autonomized discourse and what they had provisionally shelved: the referent – on nature's side – and the speaker – on the side of society/subject . . . If one autonomizes discourse by turning nature over to the epistemologists and giving up society to the sociologists, one makes it impossible to stitch these three resources (nature, discourse and society) back together again.

Nature, society and discourse are kept more or less separate from each other in an over-reaching work of purification. The mediation, networking and hybridization that goes on between them is more or less ignored – and in this move the heterogeneous materials and diverse processes through which our world is actually constructed are occluded.

The social constructionist turn in childhood studies has had just such an effect. There is widespread agreement that childhood should be understood as a historical, social and cultural phenomenon and this is counterposed to the notion that childhood is natural. An oft-quoted statement of this position came from *Constructing and Reconstructing Childhood*:

> The immaturity of children is a biological fact but the ways in which that immaturity is understood and made meaningful is a fact of culture.
>
> (Prout and James, 1990: 7)

Taken literally this posits two incommensurable realms of nature and culture. Childhood as social/cultural is understood as an effect of discourse. An even stronger statement of this perspective comes from Rex and Wendy Stainton-Rogers (1992: 6–7):

> The basic thesis . . . is very simple. We live in a world that is produced through stories – stories that we are told, stories that we recount and stories that we create.

The implication of this statement of the social constructionist view of childhood is clearly spelt out: 'we regard "childhood" as constructed through its telling . . . there can only be stories and storytellers of childhood' (Stainton-Rogers and Stainton-Rogers, 1992: 12).

Of course the insight that childhood is (in part) discursively constructed is very important. There are many extremely valuable and revealing analyses that derive from it. Showing how socially situated discursive practices apprehend and construct different aspects of childhood is a very worthwhile activity. But it stands in danger of becoming merely a reverse discourse, declaring 'society' where previously had been written 'nature'. In fact, as we will see in Chapter 4, social constructionist accounts of childhood are often more evasive than this. They bracket out biology, paying it little attention or according it only some 'last instance' role in constraining what is possible.

Equally important, because they have to divide the world into the natural and the social/cultural, they misapprehend the character of the world in which children actually grow up. Consider, for example, the following statements:

> Childhood is a social phenomenon. . .Childhood contexts and social practices are socially constructed. There is not much 'natural' about the environments in which children grow-up and spend their time: for children in Western societies mainly centred around home, classroom, and playground, as well as in cars, buses and other forms of transport, in shopping malls and discos. These are human creations that regulate children's lives.
>
> (Maybin and Woodhead, 2003)

> Cultures of childhood are profoundly social. For children in Western societies expressed through numerous shared activities: through peer group playing and games, styles of dress and behaviour, ways of talking, use of phones, mobiles, texting, internet chat rooms, patterns of consumption of commercial toys, TV, computer games and other media.
>
> (Kehily and Swann, 2003)

Both of these passages advocate a social constructionist view of childhood. In them we are asked to take artefacts such cars, phones and TVs as proof of the 'social' character of childhood. There is, we are told, nothing very 'natural' about them. A moment's reflection will show that this cannot be correct. In fact such a statement only makes sense if one wishes to separate out nature and culture, forcing all entities to belong to either one or the other. In reality there is much (but not everything) about technological artefacts that is 'natural', just as there is much (but not everything) that is 'social'. They are exactly hybrids of culture and nature.

Conclusion

My argument, then, is that the Darwinian legacy to childhood studies was to root them in biology. The tendency through the twentieth century was to add a social dimension to childhood but in a way that counterposed it to the biological and therefore asserted their separation. In the late-twentieth century, social constructionism, while conceding biological immaturity as a human universal, hailed childhood as a more or less purely social and cultural phenomenon, marked by its spatial and historical variability. Not surprisingly this new thinking gave little attention to biological aspects, preferring to bracket them off. The move to a social constructionist account of childhood, therefore, entailed making a radical disjunction between society and biology. I will argue throughout this book that such dualistic oppositions are ultimately unhelpful and do not represent a sustainable way forward for childhood studies. In later chapters I will consider how childhood might be thought of as a heterogeneous assembly in which the social, technological and biological aspects of childhood are already 'impure' entities. Before doing so, however, I will spend the next chapter looking in more detail at the contemporary sociological contribution to the study of childhood.

3   The dualities of the social

We live in a world populated by structures – a complex mixture of geolog-
ical, biological, social, and linguistic constructions that are nothing but
accumulations of materials shaped and hardened by history. Immersed as we
are in this mixture, we cannot help but interact in a variety of ways with
other historical constructions that surround us, and in these interactions we
generate novel combinations, some of which possess emergent properties. In
turn, these synergistic combinations, whether of human origin or not, become
the raw material for further mixtures. This is how the population of structures inhabiting our planet has acquired its rich variety, as the entry of novel
materials into the mix triggers wild proliferations of new forms.

(Manuel De Landa, 1997: 25)

Introduction

The construction of childhood studies around a dichotomous opposition of
culture and nature was the central theme of Chapter 2. In this chapter I
will critically review the sociological turn that childhood studies have taken
over the last period. I will consider the problems that this has created, and
suggest some new themes and directions that I believe will take the field
forward. The central problem I will discuss is familiar from the last chapter.
It is that the construction of a place for childhood within sociology was
accomplished in terms that reproduce the oppositional dichotomies around
which modernist sociology turns. These include the opposition of nature
and culture but in this chapter I will also point to the issues of structure
and agency, the individual and society, and being and becoming. The key
point I will develop is that childhood studies need to move beyond these
dichotomies and deploy non-dualistic analytical resources.

The sociology of childhood

The emergence of the sociology of childhood during the 1980s and 1990s,
although only one part of the 'social turn' of childhood studies, was a crys-
tallizing moment. Internationally, the sociology of childhood grew rapidly
and the topic was placed on the sociological agenda with a seriousness and

level of interest that it had not received before. The concept of socialization was criticized for rendering children as passive and for having an excessive focus on the individual. Because it focuses on the outcome of adulthood, it marginalizes the process of growing up and sidelines children's own actions, meanings and cultures. Developmentalism, dominant within psychological discourses of childhood, was criticized for setting up adulthood as the standard of rationality, for rendering putative stages of growth as natural, and assuming a universality to childhood which historical, social and cultural studies suggested that it does not have. Prout and James (1990/1997) synthesized a number of different critical elements in a programmatic statement for the 'new paradigm in the sociology of childhood'. I will quote its six points in their entirety:

1. Childhood is understood as a social construction. As such it provides an interpretive frame for contextualizing the early years of human life. Childhood, as distinct from biological immaturity, is neither a natural nor universal feature of human groups but appears as a specific structural and cultural component of many societies.
2. Childhood is a variable of social analysis. It can never be divorced from other variables such as class, gender, or ethnicity. Comparative and cross-cultural analysis reveals a variety of childhoods rather than a single and universal phenomenon.
3. Children's social relationships are worthy of study in their own right, independent of the perspective and concerns of adults.
4. Children must be seen as active in the construction and determination of their own social lives, the lives of those around them and of the societies in which they live. Children are not just passive subjects of social structures and processes.
5. Ethnography is a particularly useful methodology for the study of childhood. It allows children a more direct voice and participation in the production of sociological data than is usually possible through experimental or survey styles of research.
6. Childhood is a phenomenon in relation to which the double hermeneutic of the social sciences is acutely present (see Giddens, 1976). That is to say to proclaim a new paradigm of childhood sociology is also to engage in and respond to the process of reconstructing childhood in society.

(Prout and James, 1990: 8)

Underlying and informing this 'new paradigm' were a number of theoretical resources that had earlier been deployed by sociologists concerned to highlight the social character of childhood. First, it drew on the interactionist sociology, developed primarily in the US during the 1970s, which had problematized the concept of socialization as rendering chil-dren too passive (see, for example, Dreitzel, 1973). Second, in the

1980s and primarily in Europe, there was a resurgence of structural sociology that saw childhood as a permanent feature of social structure (Qvortrup *et al.*, 1994). Third, in the 1980s and in both Europe and the US, social contructionism was used to problematize and destabilize taken-for-granted concepts of childhood and subject them to a relativist gaze. This insisted on the historical and temporal specificity of childhoods and focused on their construction through discourse (see, for example, Jenks, 1982, 1990). Finally, writers such as Mayall (1994) drew on feminist studies in order to portray children as a minority group, subject to oppression by adults.

Modernist sociology

The work of creating a new sociological approach to childhood took place against the background of intensified social change discussed in Chapter 1. Older representations of childhood were being rendered inadequate by social and economic change that involved the diversification and destabilization of childhood. However, this complex, messy disordering of social life was also eroding modernist sociology in general, rendering it inadequate to late modernity. The central project of modernist sociology was the search for the principles of social order. What was it, sociologists asked, that made it possible for millions of individual humans to form coherent, stable and structured social wholes? Their answers varied widely. In Marxist sociology the answer was seen to lie in the dialectical unfolding of the mode of production that created class systems and class conflict, which (in the last instance, of course) shaped social and cultural life. The Durkheimian answer pointed to social solidarity rooted in shared norms and moral values. The Weberian highlighted processes of instrumental rationalization that created modern forms of organization in business, the state and the army. As a broad generalization, however, each of these saw 'society' as large, more or less stable blocks (usually thought of as coterminous with the nation state), ordered according to their preferred principle. In the effort to portray social life in this way it was necessary to exclude ambivalence as much as possible. The tendency was to theorize this claim through sets of dichotomous oppositions. To repeat Bauman's point (1991: 14), this created an 'obsession with separating . . . The central frame of both modern intellect and modern practice is opposition – more precisely, dichotomy'.

Modernist sociology was marked by the proliferation of dichotomies through which the social world was divided into discrete topics: structure versus agency; local versus global; identity versus difference; continuity versus change . . . and so on. But in the face of societies that had become markedly disordered and were overflowing with phenomena that were mixed, hybrid, complex, impure, ambivalent, shifting, liquid, networked then social theory was compelled to search for fresh terms of analysis. Whatever the concepts deployed, they sought to convey a sense that the neat separation of things that modernity strove for was no longer adequate to the task of understanding contemporary social life. It was, then, in the midst of this shift in the character of social life and in the middle of this crisis of social theory that the contemporary sociology of childhood had its beginnings. It came into being in relation to a sociological tradition and theoretical apparatus that had already entered a period of self-doubt, instability and re-problematization. In the 1980s and 1990s sociology was running to catch up with a complex set of social changes outlined earlier and which undermined the modernist assumptions that had informed it for most of the previous century. The problem with this from the point of childhood studies was that modernist social theory had never provided much space for childhood. The sociology of childhood was, therefore, presented with a double task: to create a space for childhood in sociological discourse; and to confront the complexity and ambiguity of childhood as a contemporary, destabilized phenomenon.

There are exceptions to this and I exaggerate the picture somewhat but my view is that the sociology of childhood is, on the whole, only just beginning to tackle the second part of this task. Rather, most effort has gone into clearing a space for childhood within modernist sociology and this has been done largely *in its own terms*. That is, it was largely accomplished within a set of dichotomized oppositions. For example, two key elements in the sociology of childhood, the agency of children and the idea of childhood as a social structural form, are drawn directly from modernist sociology in a more or less unmodified form. This has led to some strange paradoxes. At the very time when social theory was coming to terms with late modernity by decentring the subject, the sociology of childhood was valorizing the subjectivity of children. While sociology was searching for metaphors of mobility, fluidity and complexity, the sociology of childhood was raising the edifice of childhood as a permanent social structure. The sociology of childhood arrived, then, on the cusp of modernity when the social theory adequate to the transformations underway in modernity was in the process of being constituted. Childhood sociology, then, seemed to need to run in order to catch up with modernist social theory that was itself becoming disorganized by social changes that exceeded and defeated its conceptual range. So to sum up, one could say that sociology's encounter with childhood is marked by late modernity – but primarily in an ironic sense: at the very time that sociological assumptions about modernity were being eroded they arrived, late, to childhood.

The dichotomies of childhood sociology

The sociology of childhood established itself within and not beyond the oppositional dichotomies of modernist sociology. Chapter 2 took up this discussion in terms of the opposition between nature and culture. It will also be taken up in Chapter 4, which is devoted to looking at some of the biological aspects of childhood. At this stage in the argument, however, a useful approach to the nature–culture dichotomy is through a critical examination of childhood as a social construction. Like interactional sociology, social constructionism highlights a plurality of childhoods that coexist, overlap and conflict with each other. Its strength is that it draws attention to the way in which all phenomena are relationally produced. For example, adulthood and childhood are both treated as effects produced within discursive acts. Social constructionism also treats agency and structure in the same way – as effects produced within discourse. It decentres both, demanding to know how they mutually produce each other and under what conditions. Because this genre of childhood studies draws on post-structuralist writing it directly challenges the dualisms of modernist social theory and in this sense points the way to escape their dominance within the sociology of childhood.

However, it does so at an enormous cost: it grants discourse (narrative, representation, symbolization . . .) a monopoly as the medium through which social life, and therefore childhood, is constructed. Accounts of the socially constructed child always privilege discourse. Some versions are distinctly idealist about childhood while others are simply silent or vague about the material components of social life. At best there is an equivocal and uneasy evasiveness about materiality, whether this is thought of as nature, bodies, technologies, artefacts or architectures.

As we have seen, Latour (1993) argues that the dualities of modernity spring from its radical separation of culture and nature, a separation that he suggests was the historical condition for the creation of the 'natural sciences'. In this arrangement 'science' took 'nature', thought of as outside culture, as its object, whereas 'culture' and 'society', thought of as outside of nature, were left to what became the 'social sciences'. As Urry puts it: 'Until recently this academic division between the world of natural facts and one of social facts was uncontentious . . . There was presumed to be a chasm between nature and society' (Urry, 2000: 10).

This pertains directly to the sociology of childhood. One reason for the long neglect of childhood by sociology was that childhood seemed to defy the division between nature and culture. Childhood's hybrid character, part natural and part social, feels distinctly uncomfortable to the modernist mentality with its concern to dichotomize phenomena. The partial solution it found, that of ceding childhood to nature (that is to the biological and medical sciences or their extensions), held until the latter part of the twentieth century. This was encoded in sociology as the idea of social-*ization* – becoming social. Children, it implied, are of nature until made part of the social. The foundation of the sociology of childhood on the idea that childhood is a social construction is, from this point of view, revealed as a reverse discourse. It turns biological reductionism on its head and replaces it with sociological reductionism. Useful though this was as a counter to the biological reductionism of childhood as natural, it is ultimately an over-statement. What seems to be required are ways of speaking about childhood that can handle the hybridity of childhood, that can tolerate its ambiguity without lapsing very quickly into the 'purification' that dichotomies demand. But the nature–culture divide is not the only dichotomous oppo-sition that is employed in sociological analyses of childhood. Among the others that are frequently drawn are: agents and structures; individuals and society; and being and becoming.

Structure and agency

As if to enhance the separation between them, approaches that look at child-hood as a feature of social structure and those that emphasize the agency of children are often referred to as, on the one hand, the sociology of child-hood and, on the other, the sociology of children. Taken on their own both approaches have many commendable features. Thus childhood as social structure is concerned with the large-scale patterning of the childhood of a given society. In understanding this it draws attention to the shifting distri-bution of resources devoted to it. It allows for long chains of cause and effect, so that a given society's form of childhood can be shaped by phenomena that are spatially and temporally distant from it. On the problematic side, however, such an approach is most concerned with what it takes to be stable and bounded entities, most commonly the nation state, and the variations in the comparative patterns of childhood found within and between them. It is relatively uninterested in the changing character of the boundaries between nationally defined societies and the flows across these boundaries. It is untroubled by the relative decline in the power of the nation state to police its boundaries and it tends to homogenize the forms of childhood found within the boundaries that it takes for granted. It tends towards a certain mathematical formalism that is more focused on the pattern than on how it is produced and constructed and it glosses over how scale and stability are achieved. It assumes that large-scale patterns explain the action of individual and collective agents, rather than seeking to understand how a pattern of activity achieves largeness of scale or, indeed, how it achieves the stability implied by the metaphor of 'structure' (Callon and Latour, 1981).

Studies of children as agents are almost the mirror image of this. Childhoods, for here they are plural not unitary, are seen to be more diversely and locally constructed through the iterative interaction between human agents. Social life is altogether more contingent and fragile, having to be continually worked at, maintained and repaired. While large-scale patterns are acknowledged this is done rather gesturally by reference to the resources and constraints that structure 'out there' is supposed to provide. How this is accomplished is rarely accounted for in any detail. The agency of children as actors is often glossed over, taken to be an essential, virtually unmediated characteristic of humans that does not require much explanation. The real novelty of the approach is found in seeing that children may have agency at all and in the injunction of the researcher to go out and find it. This they have most successfully done.

Individual and society

This is a question that reverberates throughout discussions of childhood in many arenas, in part because it draws on and amplifies some problems of interdisciplinary working. In particular it reflects differences in the habits of thought of psychology and sociology. Psychologists tend to centre 'the individual' child and cast society as the context of the child's development. Sociologists tend to centre 'society', constituting it an object separate from but impacting on the individual. Like the dichotomized opposition of being and becoming, which I discuss below (see p. 66), the separation of the individual and the social leads to the creation of two tracks along which separate lines of enquiry run. Clearly something more is required if interdisciplinary work is to be fruitful.

It is as a solution to this problem that Bronfenbrenner's (1979) ecological model of child development, discussed in Chapter 2, was created. In it 'the child' is pictured as an individual at the centre of multiple systems. These move from the 'micro' (such as home or school), through the 'meso' (such as the local community) to the 'macro' (such as the economy or media). This approach has been taken up widely and is popular primarily because it seems to offer a solution to the problem of 'levels', an issue widely recognized across the social sciences. Although differently glossed by various disciplinary languages (in sociology, for example, by the terms 'macro' and 'micro'), this refers to the fact that social phenomena can rarely be understood only by reference to entities within the immediate vicinity of the action. There is also, so to speak, some sort of 'action at a distance', when entities remote from a locale shape or influence what occurs there. Bronfenbrenner provides a simple, graphic and flexible way of dealing with this problem. Briefly stated, the social–ecological approach makes the assumption that development is a reciprocal process of interaction and accommodation across the life cycle involving the individual in increasingly large contexts. Although depicted as separate circles, users of this approach are urged to think of it as entailing reciprocity and interaction between individuals and their multiple environments.

However, despite this encouragement to examine the interaction between levels, most social science continues to deal with children by focusing on one level only. For example, a lot of attention may be given to the 'micro' and the rest is dealt with as a more or less constant 'context'. Alternatively the wider context is studied but the linkages between this and local circumstances and practices are left unexamined or assumed. What often emerges is what has been termed 'multi-level' (rather than cross-level) research, in which text and context, foreground and background are dealt with as if they were separate spheres, when what is needed is exactly the dynamic interplay between them (Shinn and Rapkin, 2000). Thus, while bidirectional reciprocity between levels is urged, it is in practice often left unconceptualized and unexamined. When it is done it is often done in such a way that context is reduced to a supposedly objective, static and relatively crude set of indices such as demographic variables (Linney, 2000).

For these reasons I believe that the ecological approach, although an advance in that it poses some essential questions, does not adequately deal with the issue of context. One might say that it is a good diagram of the problem – but not of the solution. It highlights the need to look at the interactions and mediations between different spheres (which, misleadingly in my view, it calls 'levels') but provides few conceptual tools for doing so. Its focus is not on what connects the different spheres of social life, or indeed how, if at all, they are constituted as separate, but on the spheres ('levels') themselves. This not only renders the spheres rather static but also takes the existence of these spheres as given rather than produced through practice within certain historically circumscribed conditions.

Being and becoming

The dichotomy between children as becomings and children as beings has been central to recent debates in the sociology of childhood. For some writers in the new sociology of childhood this has been constructed as an opposition, often dogmatically insisted upon, such that they deny the possibility of considering children as both beings and becomings. For others this was always a troublesome opposition. Christensen (1994) pointed out that the being/becoming distinction was only useful if children's 'being' was understood as lived in time, with a remembered past and an anticipated future. Being, she suggested, could not be timeless. Nick Lee (2001a) has recently argued, conclusively to my mind, that the sociology of childhood needs to recognize both being and becoming. First, he suggests that although the opposition made sense from the standpoint of modernist societies, it has become unsustainable in the face of recent changes in employment and family. The trends discussed in Chapter 1 have also re-shaped adulthood. It is no longer expected that adults will necessarily enter into one lifelong marriage or pursue one career until their retirement. We live in the era of 'reconstituted families', 'lifelong education' and 'reskilling'. These have made the 'unfinished' character of adult lives as visible as those of children. Both adults and children can be seen in these terms as becomings without compromising the need to respect their status as beings or persons. Second, by emphasizing children as beings 'in their own right' the new sociology of childhood risks endorsing the myth of the autonomous and independent person, as if it were possible to be human without belonging to a complex web of interdependencies. Lee therefore critiques the new sociology of childhood for one-sidedly basing itself on the idea of children as beings. Rather, both children and adults should be seen through a multiplicity of becomings in which all are incomplete and dependent.

Strategies towards an included middle

These examples illustrate the problematic ways in which dichotomous oppositions are routinely employed in the sociology of childhood. Furthermore, dualistic formulations are highly resistant to change even when the problem is recognized. The deconstructive sociologies of Giddens, Elias and Bourdieu try, and partially succeed, in overcoming the division of structure and agency – but in the practice and output of childhood sociologists the dualism reappears over and over again, while in psychology the use of multilevel approaches has not succeeded in tracking how the 'macro' enters into and is part of the 'micro'. Childhood sociologists ground themselves in the 'being' of children but find this ground slipping from under their feet as the distinction between adulthood and childhood is itself rendered more uncertain. Above all, the nature–culture distinction is itself quite inadequate to the increasingly hybrid character of the contemporary world.

This is not to say that work based on these oppositions has not yielded insights. Quite the contrary, the sociology of childhood has been a very fruitful enterprise, opening up many new questions, inspiring hundreds of empirical studies and exerting an influence in the way many other academic disciplines have looked at children. But, however successful the programme outlined in the 'new paradigm' has been, it is, I think, now running up against the limits of its possibilities. A number of childhood sociologists have recognized these problems. Thorne, suggesting the need for reflection and renewal, recently remarked that the 'new' sociology of childhood is now actually becoming rather middle-aged (Thorne, 2000). German sociologists of childhood devoted their 2002 meeting in Berlin to discussing ways of revivifying the social study of childhood, a field they sense is faltering and has lost its way. At the same time critical voices, both internal (for example, Alanen, 2001a; Lee, 2001a) and external (for example, Buckingham, 2000), are being raised. It seems, then, that after more than two decades of extraordinarily creative effort, leading to new theoretical, methodological and empirical insights, the new sociology of childhood is increasingly troubled.

This trouble is, in the first place, theoretical. The analytical categories that childhood sociologists use are largely dichotomous. They are constructed around an either/or logic of mutual exclusion at a time when childhood seems to be, on the contrary, becoming more ambiguous and more diverse. It is increasingly difficult to bracket out the empirically generated diverse and hybrid character of childhood and the shifting boundaries between childhood and adulthood. When the theoretical terms used to grasp these entities are built on mutual exclusion they become increasingly unable to find any empirical purchase. It is hard to find any point of communication between the polar terms of the analysis because they are defined (and in their discursive logic, define themselves) as outside of each other's domain. To be meaningful they seem to need to be pure and the continual effort to purify them means either deleting all that mediates them or distributing it between polar terms of analysis so that they become the property of one or the other. This directs attention away from the mediations and connections between the oppositions they erect. In this sense they exclude all that lies beneath and between them, effacing their mutual dependence and occluding important features about the way in which contemporary childhoods are constructed.

What sort of strategy, then, is needed to overcome these problems and move the field on? Two possible ways are to be found in the literature, but neither of them is really adequate to the task. The first might be called *peaceful coexistence* (which is, of course, another term for cold war). At its happiest this has meant allowing different sociologies of childhood, located at different poles of a dichotomy, to run on separate tracks with only minimal effort being made to explore the territory that connects them. The problem with this is that it is not so much a solution as a shelving of the issue. It is somewhat in this vein that Qvortrup writes. Himself an advocate of what he calls the 'macro-structural' approach, he recognizes that the 'microscopical' is important too. Ideally they should be made to coincide but:

> there are no good reasons to argue about the paramouncy [*sic*] of either a micro- or macro-level approach; neither is it demanded that each and everybody must in his or her research capture all levels. The choice is partly made by inclination and/or temperament.
>
> (Qvortrup, 2000: 93)

It is certainly true that arguing that big things are more important than small things is fruitless. But why do we have to accept that there are only two registers of scale, macro and micro, in the world? To make the world look like this we have to convert a gradient, that is the whole range of scales on which entities exist, into a dualism. In doing so we tend to diminish the entities that mediate between the two and we miss the processes by which small becomes big and big becomes small.

The second strategy could be called *heuristic play*. This is more or less the approach suggested by James *et al.* (1998). In *Theorizing Childhood* we accounted for the different approaches to the sociology of childhood by locating them within the set of dualisms that we took as characterizing the mainstream of sociological theory: agency and structure; identity and difference; continuity and change; locality and globality. We argued that the way in which these dualisms have been selected, traversed and deployed by analysts of childhood have shaped what we saw as four main genres of childhood sociology. In so doing we found ourselves having to insist that, contrary to appearances, 'our purpose is not to generate a separatist typology . . . we are concerned to provide an analytic framework that will consolidate the new social studies of childhood and provide pointers for its development' (James *et al.*, 1998. 206). Having thus formalized the separation between genres, we then resort to calling for childhood sociologists to be playful with them, finding new points of connection and intersection between them. Again, this strategy has not been unproductive – and indeed playing with the theoretical possibilities is what much very good empirical research does in the face of complex realities. However, by making our main point of reference one focused on the dualistic discourse of sociology we risked entrenching the sociology of childhood within them and thus limiting the ground on which the field could move forward.

Resources for an included middle

If these two approaches are inadequate, then I suggest there is a need to develop and explore new ideas. These ideas should be concerned with and help us to include the excluded middle of dichotomies that have been made to be oppositional. In other words, they should not already inscribe a set of dichotomies within the field but see childhood as a complex phenomenon not readily reducible to one end or the other of a polar separation. I am not here advocating some indeterminate 'middle way'. The approach I have in mind is similar to the Italian writer Norberto Bobbio who talks of the 'included middle'. This, to quote him:

> attempts to find its own space between two opposites and, although it inserts itself between them, it does not eliminate them . . . [they] cease to be two mutually exclusive totalities like two sides of the same coin that cannot both be seen at the same time.
>
> (Bobbio, 1996: 7)

What sort of analytical language would it be useful to employ when talking about the diverse and shifting orderings of childhood that the contemporary world presents to us? As I have already suggested the sociology of childhood as it is presently constituted offers us a choice between three problematic options. One is a set of metaphors like 'childhood as structure', 'system' and 'order' that emphasize large-scaleness, stability and determinism. Another, deriving from interactionism, offers notions of childhood as a local, negotiated order. This emphasizes the work of agents but often tends too much towards voluntarism. Another choice is presented by postmodernism, which eschews notions of stability seeing only fluidity and constant change. Although this opens up important aspects of social life, especially the role of discourse, it is, to put it mildly, less good at handling questions of materiality. However, the problems faced by the social study of childhood are not unique to it. In fact they traverse the whole of social analysis, whatever its empirical focus. The tendency for contemporary social life to be marked by dissolving boundaries and height-ened ambiguity is a general one and, partly in response to it, new frame-works for understanding the world after modernity are being brought into existence. It is by utilizing these that I believe the study of childhood can make its next steps.

Actor–network theory

Actor–network theory (ANT) offers one such possibility. ANT is a form of relational materialism. It is concerned with the materials from which social life is produced and the processes by which these are brought into relationship with each other. Because it wishes to avoid a priori assump-tions about what these materials and means are, actor–network theory is sceptical about many commonly employed forms of sociological explana-tion, especially those that mobilize ready-made abstractions, for example 'power' and 'organization'. From an actor–network viewpoint these are not explanations but phenomena in need of explanation. It is argued that:

> If we want to understand the mechanics of power and organisation it is important not to start *assuming* whatever we wish to explain . . . If we do this we close off most of the interesting questions about the *origins* of power and organisation . . . [instead] we might ask how some kinds of interactions succeed in stabilizing and reproducing themselves: how is it that they overcome resistance and seem to become 'macro-social'; how is it that they seem to generate the effects such as power, fame, size, scope, or organisation with which we are all familiar.
>
> (Law, 1992: 380)

This approach has much in common with other forms of sociological analysis which emphasize the relational, constructed and processual char-acter of social life; actor–network therefore draws on semiotics, social constructionism and symbolic interactionism, while being quite distinct from each of them in certain crucial respects. One key difference is that, although it accepts the importance of discourse, actor–network is thor-oughly materialist. Another is that it rejects the assumption that society is constructed through human action and meaning alone. 'Society' is seen as produced in and through patterned networks of heterogeneous materials; it is made up through a wide variety of shifting associations (and dissocia-tions) between human *and* non-human entities. Indeed, so ubiquitous are associations between humans and the rest of the material world that all entities are to be seen as hybrids – what Latour (1993) has termed 'quasi-objects' and 'quasi-subjects' – where the boundary between the human and the non-human is shifting, negotiated and empirical. Social life cannot, therefore, be reduced either to the 'purely' human or to the 'purely' technological (or animal, vegetable, mineral, abstract . . .). Neither the human nor the technological determines the overall patterning or ordering that results from their combination. Approaches that try to make one *or* the other do all the explanatory work result in reductionism.

The lineage of this position can be traced in the development of the social study of technology, from within which actor–network theory emerged. This started with the notion that technology could be seen as 'impacting' on society, a position which relied on an unsustainable technology–society dualism. The counter to this position, that technology is shaped by social relations, maintains the dualism (see, for example, MacKenzie and Wajcman, 1985). As this literature developed it became clear that no hard and fast distinction between 'social relations' and 'technology' could be made. Laboratories and design departments, for example, are already hybrid phenomena within which the 'technological' and the 'social' relations are mutually constitutive and inextricable. They are, so to speak, 'embedded' in each other, each constituting and shaping the other (Bijker and Law, 1994; Callon, 1986). From this insight a more rigorously monistic strand of thought, called actor–network theory, has developed. This proposes an expanded form of semiotics in which both human and non-human entities participate. The aim of this is to explore the processes by and through which human and non-human entities involved in social life relate to each other.

Although ANT began in the sociology of science and technology, its non-dualistic approach has proved useful in relation to a much wider range of empirical phenomena (see, for example, Law, 1994; Law and Hassard, 1999). Using the metaphor of 'network' it suggests that childhood could be seen as a collection of different, sometimes competing and sometimes conflicting, heterogeneous orderings. These can be fragile but they can also be stabilized, become widespread and, therefore, found on a large scale. Network seems to offer a language of ordering that stands between the polar oppositions offered by modernist social theory. For example, ANT has a useful way of avoiding the opposition of agency and structure. First it insists that actors can be of many different kinds: human as in the case of children and adults but also non-human ones such as organisms, artefacts and technologies. All of these are treated as hybrids of culture and nature produced through networks of connection and disconnection. Second, this means that actors come in all sizes from small ones like the individual child to large ones like the State or a media company. This is because all actors are understood as networks even though they may appear and act as points. Behind every actor, whether a child or the State or a media company, lies a complex, more or less held together network of people and things. 'Actor-networks' that are stabilized appear like the solid objects that modernist sociology liked to call 'structure' or 'system'. But such networks can become fragile and are always partial and defeasible. New networks can arise that may fall by the wayside but may also stabilize and grow in scale. In other words new forms of childhood arise when new sets of network connections, for example between children and technologies such as TV and the internet, are made. Such new networks may overlap and coexist with older ones but they may also conflict. A key question, therefore, is what makes up the network that produces a particular form of childhood?

Complexity and non-linear systems

When sociologists speak about childhood as a permanent feature of the social structure (or, as we will see below, think of childhood as part of a 'generational order'), they are pointing to the stability of childhood as a social institution. The implication is that childhood is worthy of serious study (only?) because it is not a temporary phenomenon but is stable and durable. This manner of speaking mirrors that found in the natural sciences where terms such as the 'structures of the atom' and the 'solar system' do the same sort of work. However, over the last 40 years the idea of structure or system in the natural sciences has undergone a revolution in thinking. The label under which these ideas are gathered together is 'complexity theory'. Furthermore, although complexity theory started in the natural sciences, in recent times it has been taken up within the social sciences (see, for example, Byrne, 1998; Eve *et al.*, 1997). Its appeal for social scientists lies in the fact that complexity theory is designed to aid the understanding of 'non-linear systems'. Non-linearity is a key characteristic of social life, at scales stretching from the individual person to global society.

The beginnings of complexity theory can be found in the realization, arrived at in the 1960s, that the assumptions, expressed in Laws of Thermodynamics, that scientists had been making about physical and chemical systems were inadequate. The chemist Ilya Prigogine pointed out that classical physics' account of energy flows in systems assumed that these systems were closed (for a useful account of his ideas, see University of Texas, 2003). It is assumed that there is no 'leakage' out of the system and no external inputs into it. In such closed systems the total amount of energy is conserved and so they tend towards equilibrium. Although such a system is not static, it is homeostatic. Any changes that occur are 'damped' down and tend to bring the system back to its basic or ground state. Such a system has limits out of which it never strays.

However, once it is allowed that systems may be open, in other words that there may be flows of energy in and out of the system, then a whole new set of possibilities becomes apparent. Complexity theory is the name given to the study of such systems. These systems do not necessarily settle into a state of equilibrium but can shift between different states, known as 'phase spaces'. This concept describes the behaviour of a whole system over time and can thus be seen as a sort of diagram or map of a system's long-term behaviour. 'Dissipative systems', as they are termed, have the ability to store imported energy (or information) by integrating it into their internal structures or exporting it into their environment. These processes render systems inherently evolutionary. They necessarily change because their internal structure is in constant development and because they are in a dynamic relationship with their environment. Their internal and external boundaries are constantly shifting. Such systems, therefore, always have to be understood over time. For various reasons beyond the scope of my discussion here, these developments over time take place in ways that are non-reversible. They have to be seen as not just changing but rather as having a complex and evolving but not goal-driven history. Once they had been identified, non-linear systems have been found to occur rather commonly. Perhaps the most widely discussed is the global climate system but the range is very wide: for example, biological evolution, the ecology of animal and plant populations, economic systems, and many aspects of social life.

In fact, complexity theorists have concentrated on four kinds of phase spaces as common outcomes of these processes. The first possibility describes a system that has long-term stability. It tends to gravitate to a point of equilibrium, where it settles into a steady state. The second is radically different from this. In it a system oscillates between two states, periodically moving from one to another. In the third, the system repeats itself according to some more complex rhythm. In the fourth, the system becomes 'chaotic' – that is its trajectory of development becomes erratic and unpredictable.

These systems are thought to have a number of important properties. The first of these is that they are *non-linear*. The classical laws of thermodynamics are a good example of a linear model. The basic idea is that the relationship between the variables of pressure, volume and temperature in a system (for example, a pressure cooker or steam turbine) is one of cause and effect. Understanding how these variables affect each other is a matter of finding out how a given unit of change in one aspect of the system (say pressure) changes the other two. By conducting experiments it becomes possible to predict how the cause and effect in a system takes place. Writ large this is the general picture provided by the Newtonian 'clockwork universe' in which, once set running, the system ticks on in the same predictable way.

Many phenomena work in this way. Much of our built environment, for example the calculations used in determining the strength of materials needed in a bridge, depends on this predictability. However, the problem with this picture as a general way of understanding the world is that many natural and social systems do not operate in this simple, linear way. In the first place they tend to have a large number of different variables working together. As noted above, weather systems are influenced by a very large number of factors. In principle, if all these could be identified and all the linear relationships between all the factors measured accurately then it would seem to be possible to predict the outcome. But there is another much more important problem. It is that each of the factors making up the weather is influenced by all of the others. The variables are in constant dynamic interplay. There are feedback and feed-forward loops between the different factors, and so-called 'second order' feedback loops between the feedback loops – stretching into an infinite recurse of complexity. Hence the hapless weather forecaster who, despite having some of the most powerful computers on earth, cannot predict the next day's weather with complete accuracy. And standing alongside the weather forecaster we might find the even more hapless social scientist grappling with the perhaps even more complex phenomenon of childhood.

A second important feature of complex systems is that small differences can have big effects. In particular the trajectory of the system over time is very sensitive to small changes in their starting conditions. Small differences at one point, or changes at a point of time in the history of the system, can produce big changes in the outcome. These magnification effects mean that even systems with the same starting conditions can become radically different over time. Such trajectories mean that systems in motion can enter a state of perturbation that results in a split or *bifurcation*. A bifurcation occurs when a system passes through a critical threshold that is non-reversible. It moves from one phase space to another. This concept has been used to understand phenomena as varied as volcanic explosions, the emergence of new species and the differentiation of neighbourhoods into multiply deprived and relatively prosperous ones. In the last example, Byrne (1998) shows that if the key parameters of a system (for example, in the case of a neighbourhood, the level of unemployment) are changed beyond those needed to keep the system stable then it enters a chaotic phase. In this condition very small differences can bring about large changes. Feedback in such systems tends to be positive, in the sense that it reinforces a direction of change rather than damping it down. One area of a town can find itself on a downward spiral, while another very similar area can survive intact.

Complex systems are self-organizing and have emergent properties. The overall shape of a complex system (its phase space) is not imposed on the system externally but emerges from the interactions between elements in the system and from the system's interactions with its environment. The system is not a superordinate entity over and above, and bearing down on, the interactions going on within it and with its wider environment. Rather its systematic character emerges from these interactions. This makes the notion of system found in complexity theory different from deterministic ones. For example, structural–functionalist approaches in sociology have been widely criticized for presenting social action as an effect of structure – that is structure as a determinant cause. This presents a rather conservative account in which 'society' determines the actions of people and discourages change.

The idea of system in complexity theory, however, is potentially much more open-ended than this. In the first place, although the overall shape of a system (that is its phase space) is predictable, the trajectory of any given individual part of it (be it an atom, an animal, or a human person) can vary very widely and is not predictable. Second, systems do not have only one possible ground state but can move between states. It has been found that, for a given system, not all factors at play within it have equal weight. When certain of these, called the control parameters, pass through critical values they bring about change in the whole system. The control parameters change because the external environment changes or because there is an interplay between the environment and internal features of the system. As systems approach such bifurcation points (when they change their form) they become very sensitive to small changes. This is because in these conditions interactions within the system can amplify small changes through positive feedback loops. So change in the parameters can tip a system towards other states (such as the cyclical or rhythmic patterns mentioned above) or they can push the system towards a series of wild oscillations until the system becomes chaotic.

Complexity theory offers an account of a system that avoids many of the dualistic problems that are encountered in current social studies of childhood. Seen through its lens, the idea of childhood as a social structure takes on a different meaning. Their systemic properties are emergent and intimately linked to the agency of the entities that populate them. Such structures of childhood may, within certain limits, be relatively stable over time but they are never static. They are always in motion and, under certain conditions, can shift from one phase state to another – or even become extremely unpredictable. In other words, complex systems have a history; they have, and cannot help but have, both being and becoming.

Generational relations

Both ANT and complexity theory seem to me to offer useful conceptual resources for the study of childhood, and in the rest of this chapter I will examine their potential through a discussion of current debates in social studies of childhood. It is notable that the problem of dichotomous opposition is already receiving attention within these. Primarily this discussion is taking place around the concept of 'generational relations' put forward by Alanen (2001a) and, in a rather different form, by Qvortrup (1994). This approach seeks to establish the idea of a 'generational system' or 'order' that is parallel to the notions of class order or gender order often employed by sociologists in speaking about social structure. In this definition generation is seen as the system of relationships in which the positions of 'child' and that of 'adult' are produced. Alanen (2001a: 12) writes of generation that it can be thought of as:

> a socially constructed system of relationships among social positions in which children and adults are the holders of specific social positions

defined in relation to each other and constituting in turn, specific (and in this case generational) structures.

In this respect the structural idea of generation is less explicitly concerned with change over time than is the well-established use of the term by Mannheim (1952/1927). While Mannheim is explicitly historical, looking at the diachronic process of generational formation, Alanen's concept is synchronic. It focuses on the pattern of relationships between adults and children as they form a more or less enduring and stable feature of social systems. The research questions that this approach, therefore, prioritizes are concerned with 'detecting the both direct and indirect, invisible relations through which children are firmly embedded in structured sets of social relations that are larger than their very immediate local relations and potentially extending as far as the global social system' (Alanen, 2001b: 142). This, it is argued, can be done by studies that examine the everyday lives of children in terms, *inter alia*, of practices of 'generationing' and by examining how, in the formation of particular versions of childhood, social, cultural and material resources are deployed and become available.

Such a position is in many respects compatible with the prospectus that I argue for in this book. It is concerned with the 'excluded middle' because it makes a shift from seeing childhood as an essentialized category to one produced within a set of relations. It is parallel to feminist sociology's move from a focus on 'women' to a concern with 'gender'. In this sense it focuses on the relations within which both childhood and adulthood are produced. It is also, in principle, interested in both the discursive and material resources, and the practices that are involved in the construction of childhood. In this sense it is at least open to the hybrid character of childhood that ANT highlights. However, so far at least, the non-human component of such a hybrid notion of generation has not received much attention in the literature on generational order. It has been discussed as if it were a 'social', i.e. purely human, construct. In Chapters 4 and 5, I will explore a view of generational relations that moves towards a view of child–adult relations that draws explicitly on their heterogeneous construction through a wide variety of social, biological and technological elements.

There are, however, a number of other problems with the idea of generational order that also need to be addressed. First, a certain amount of confusion arises from using a vocabulary of 'generation' in ways quite different from their widely known meanings in the writings of Mannheim, which, though dating from the 1920s, continue as an active research tradition, especially in Germany (see Corsten, 2003), and have been very influential in the field of youth studies. Their main focus is temporal. Embedded in a wider concern to explain social and cultural change, Mannheim's approach sees 'generations' as social units that come into existence when a cohort of people, born around the same time, grow up experiencing the same social and historical events and come to see themselves as a distinct generational group sharing common experience, values and attitudes. Mannheim explores the social factors that make this emergence possible but also suggests that, once in existence, a 'generation' has an effect of its own on processes of social and historical change. He draws a distinction between 'generation in itself' and 'generation for itself'. The former refers to the fact that a cohort was born into similar social and historical circumstances (the so-called 'generational location'). The latter refers to the possibility that the cohort members may come to think of and identify themselves as a distinct group. The main topics of empirical concern in this tradition are, therefore, the periodization of birth circumstances (in terms of their social and historical particularities) and the discovery of whether, in fact, a given cohort does develop a sense of itself as a distinct 'generation'.

It can be seen immediately that the Mannheimian perspective raises very different issues and research questions from those suggested by the structural and, in tendency at least, synchronic notions of Qvortrup and Alanen. For the latter, generation is a phenomenon of social structure rendered necessary once the distinction between adults and children becomes established. For Mannheim, whether or not a generation exists is an empirical and contingent question. Furthermore, in Mannheim a generation comes into existence partly because it creates a shared identity but the possibility of being a member of a generation is governed and bounded by being born during a particular period of history. However, in the structural sense all children at *any and all* points of time form the childhood end of a system of generational relations. Confusion is, therefore, created by mixing up these two different approaches, confusion that is avoided to some extent by recognizing their rather different implications.

However, Alanen's formulations, taken entirely on their own terms, also give rise to some problems. First, her idea of generational order seems to restrict the range of relationships that children are seen as having. There are only two subject positions: adult and child. Alanen, in contrast to Qvortrup, is insistent that the childhood–adulthood relationship arises from an 'internal', logical necessity rather than from any 'external' contingencies. She is critical of Qvortrup for implying that generational relationships are formed in part through historical contingencies. However, this seems to me to be unnecessarily abstract and scholastic. It is too restrictive about the range of 'generational phenomena' that might be found. Empirically speaking it is possible to find a spectrum of subject positions (for example, 'infant', 'teenager', 'young adult' and, more recently, 'tweenie') that are produced through generationing processes. These are partly explained through the wide range of empirical factors (such as technologies and consumption practices) that play a part in creating generational effects. Furthermore, Alanen's approach reinstates childhood as part of an oppositional, binary system. It turns around the adulthood–childhood difference and is therefore centred on inter-generational relationships. Because of this it is difficult to see how intra-generational relationships can be properly acknowledged. Such intra-generational relations are themselves very diverse, only very inadequately captured through the term peer relations. Nevertheless, there are good arguments and good evidence that these intra-generational relations, peer or otherwise, play an important part in children's lives (see, for example, Corsaro, 1997; Frønes, 1995).

Third, in both Alanen's and Qvortrup's formulations, the concept of generation deploys a language of system or structure that tends to over-emphasize the stability and solidity of inter-generational relations. As a consequence it tends to fall back into the idea of a single generational structure of which all empirical variations are merely instances. 'Generation' thus comes to resemble an irreducible 'block' of social order. The process of 'generationing', the active side of the theory, therefore loses some of its potential as an open-ended process, constructed through the effects of all kinds of heterogeneity and contingency, able to move in unexpected directions and produce new kinds of generational phenomena.

Actor–network and complexity theory offer ways of thinking about generational ordering that help to avoid these problems. Both would treat 'generational orderings' as phenomena that need explaining rather than necessarily carrying explanatory power themselves. Both would point to the heterogeneous materials from which 'generation' is produced. Both would keep the processes of generationing open-ended and the plurality and range of 'generational orderings' emergent and open to enquiry. The risk of turning generation from a process into a finished product is reduced if ordering is thought of as an emergent property. It becomes possible to think of generational ordering as producing different 'phase states' in generational relationships – not only stability but also bifurcations and periods of instability or chaos. De Landa (1997), for example, argues that in very complex systems, such as those found in human history, the elements from which trajectories are formed may combine with each other so as to produce novel new properties more intensely than is the case in natural systems. De Landa applies what he calls 'non-linear combinatronics' to a range of phenomena, such as the dynamics of cities and language change, over the last millenium of history. His approach could also be applied to generational relationships to show how they have emerged, transformed and pluralized over time.

Life course and heterogeneous becoming

In a recent study Mannion and I'Anson (2003) use the framework of generational relations to understand children's participation in an arts organization. The organization had a special remit to cater for children and young people and a reputation for involving young people's participation, and was therefore of special interest from the generational perspective. The researchers tracked the process through which children participated in

the redesigning of the physical space of the arts centre. They treat generational relations as open-ended, contingent and emergent products of plays
between heterogeneous elements – material, cultural, spatial, discursive and
so on. It is these, they suggest, rather than the mysterious workings of an
underlying but invisible and necessary structure of generation that produced
the generational relations they found. The study shows how, in finding new
ways of working together, the adults and children not only reconfigured
the space and the material organization of the place but that, as part and
parcel of this, adult–child identifications, relations and the associated
constructions of adulthood and childhood were also transformed. Far from
being stable and fixed, generational relations within this context changed as
the heterogeneous processes at play in the setting created new effects and
new relationships. The authors use an open-ended, non-teleological notion
of becoming, commenting that: 'Instead of just emphasising that children
are beings too, we have shown the fruitfulness of considering *both adult and
child* as partial becomings' (Mannion and I'Anson, 2003: 21).

Paying attention to 'becoming' in this way also suggests the usefulness
to the study of childhood of another relational concept – that of the life
course (see Giele and Elder, 1998). Life course analysis is a broad topic,
encompassing historical time (generations and cohorts), individual time (life
history and biography) and institutional time (careers, sequences and transitions). In all three approaches the life course is understood as a sequence
of stages or status configurations and transitions in life which are culturally
and institutionally framed from birth to death.

With some provisos, this also seems to me to constitute a useful framework for advancing studies of children's relationships (see Elder *et al.*, 1993.
My reasons for thinking this flow from the position I have argued so far.
First, it builds on the critique internal to childhood studies of an exclusive
focus on children's being that was always troublesome (Christensen, 1994).
Second, a life-course approach allows for the multiplicity and complexity
of childhoods. It does not reduce the phenomenon to a logical or internal
relationship between just two terms – adult and child. It recognizes just
what Alanen seems to want to exclude – that is the importance of external
contingencies in the shaping of particular childhoods. It emphasizes that life
courses are open to the effect of a wide range of human and non-human
factors in constructing multiple versions of childhood and adulthood as they
shift through time.

As we have seen, Latour uses the term 'heterogeneous networks of the
social' to indicate such complex forms and content within which human
life is constituted (Latour, 1993: 6). Such shifting networks of heterogeneous
elements span the life course in combinations that are empirically varied but
do not in principle demand different kinds of analysis. There is no need in
this respect to arbitrarily separate children from adults, as if they were some
different species of being. Rather the task is to see how different versions

of child or adult emerge from the complex interplay, networking and orchestration of different natural, discursive, collective and hybrid materials.

One problem with the conventional life-course approach is that it often brackets childhood as a single stage. However, in a recent study about children and food, Christensen (2003) treats childhood as an interlocking series of socially and culturally constituted phases rather than a single stage of the life course. These phases are defined by the shifting goals, values and interests of children as well as their changing social position. This analysis respects how children see themselves as 'growing up' but also recognises children's individual and collective negotiation of the different phases of childhood, as these are constructed through their encounters with structures and practices in the family, school and other institutions. Children's focus on competencies around food shift according to these phases. At different times children are shown to focus on the practical skills of handling food and tools, having likes and dislikes, being able to provide for oneself and others, and being distinctive in one's individual style and taste.

A good deal of research has emphasized how important it is to recognize that 'growing up' is not accomplished individually but collectively – that is within a set of peer relations. For example, Corsaro (1996) shows how children work out together how to accomplish key institutional transitions, such as that from pre-school to school. Thorne (1993) has shown that relationships between children are mobile and fast moving, recentering quickly around many different dimensions of identity and difference. Frønes (1995), in particular, has argued that peer relations, which are communicatively complex but equal, develop the competencies of expressiveness, closeness and community. However, we also need to be careful not to limit children's relationships with each other to the category of peers. It is a rather imprecise term and one that would be unacceptable in the analysis of adult relationships – exactly because it tends to elide very different kinds of relations, ranging from those of work, of neighbourhood and of friendship. It tends to simplify and give a coherence to children's relationships with each other that may be misleading. It misses out, for example, relationships between older and younger children, and those between children and non-kin significant adults such as neighbours. A life-course perspective, understood in terms of heterogeneity and complexity, can however, contain all this variation because it moves between historical time, individual time and institutional time. It shows how institutional frameworks can both construct and impede relationships between children. Peer relations, for instance, are made possible by putting same-age children together in the same class but a friendship between an older and younger child is impeded when one moves to secondary school and the other does not.

Mobilities

Once social life is recognized as heterogeneous then the a priori parcelling out of entities (people, adults, children, bodies, minds, artefacts, animals, plants, architectures, etc.) into culture or nature becomes unthinkable. Social phenomena must be comprehended as complex entities in which a medley of culture and nature is given as a condition of their possibility. There are no more pure entities, only the hybrids that Latour refers to as 'quasi-subjects' and 'quasi-objects'. This, it hardly needs saying, is much more analytically challenging than starting with a given division between sets of oppositional dualities such as nature and culture. There is no need in this respect to arbitrarily separate children from adults, as if they were some different species of being. Rather the task is to see whether and how different versions of child or adult emerge from the complex inter-play, networking and orchestration of different natural, discursive, collective and hybrid materials. Shifting networks of heterogeneous elements are involved in the construction of generational relationships and the life course. These constructions can be understood as complex non-linear systems. In some instances the generational relations that they produce are relatively stable. At other times, when new elements enter into the networks through which they are constituted, they begin to shift. The picture of childhood change in the context of globalization presented in Chapter 1 becomes comprehensible in terms of such heterogeneous complexity.

A key feature of these processes, however, is heightened mobility. Global networks are alive with flows of ideas, people and things. The locales of childhood and the (inter- and intra-) generational relationships of children can be seen as products of the flows that traverse them. I argued earlier that it is precisely this issue of flows and mobilities that the ecological model of childhood proposed by Bronfenbrenner is poor at handling. The 'micro', 'meso' and 'macro' levels are treated as if they were different containers within which children are held. As Thorne puts it:

> Bronfenbrenner asserted that these separate contexts are 'linked' and, in turn, 'nested' within broader 'macrosystems' of ideology and institutional structure. But his relatively static framework tends to constrain rather than facilitate understanding of the complex and processual dynamics of social life. It also runs the risk of drawing on common-sense American typifications of sites like 'family', 'school', and 'neighbourhood' rather than opening towards the enormous range of contingent circumstances in which children grow up.
>
> (2004, forthcoming: 1)

The approach I advocate here, therefore, is concerned to look at the locales of childhood not as 'containers' but as places constructed through flows of heterogeneous materials. Schools, for example, are related to other schools, to households, playgrounds, after-school clubs, firms, local authorities, trades unions, ministries, courts and so on. People cross these boundaries bringing with them different and conflicting ideas, experiences, ideals, values and visions (all the things that make up discourses) and different material resources. Things also pass across the boundaries and play no less a part. These include texts, such as the curriculum guidelines, teaching materials, letters laying down funding policy and so on; and machines (such as computers) that work in this way rather than that, or facilitate that rather than this possibility for learning and so on. The hybrid 'actants', people and things, that flow in and between different settings all play a part in constructing what emerges as 'childhood' and 'adulthood' there. It is by tracing these flows that we can come to understand them better.

Conclusion

In this chapter I have drawn attention to the heterogeneous materials and practices from which a potentially large (depending on the time used) stream of 'childhoods' and 'adulthoods' are generated. I have argued that these processes cannot be understood through a conceptual apparatus that constantly strains towards dualistic oppositions. This is not to argue that there are no disjunctures, distinctions or even dichotomies among the phenomena with which childhood studies are concerned. Obviously there are. For example, the distinction between children and adults, although weakening in recent times, is a real (but constructed) distinction. The point is that such differences are themselves the product of heterogeneous processes. To understand how they emerge we also have to pay attention to the included middle. The languages of non-linearity, hybridity, network and mobility are important if we are concerned to do this because they are less likely to recapitulate the oppositional dichotomies of modernist social theory. In this respect they are more in keeping with the destabilization and pluralization of both childhood and adulthood that mark our times. In short it is part of the 'step from modernity' that the study of childhood has now to make.

4   Childhood, nature and culture

> It will not do to approach science as social or cultural construction, as if culture and society were transcendent categories, any more than nature or the object is. Outside the premises of enlightenment – i.e. of the modern – the binary pairs of culture and nature, science and society, the technical and the social all lose their constitutive, oppositional quality. Neither can explain the other.
>
> (Haraway, 1990: 7)

Introduction

By the last two decades of the twentieth century there was widespread agreement that childhood should be understood as a historical, social and cultural phenomenon. Generally speaking this social and cultural take on childhood was contrasted to the biological one inherited from childhood study's modern beginnings in Darwin. To be sure, both psychology and paediatrics developed various additive views, in which a debate about nature–nurture revolved around the differing proportions of each that were to go into the mixture. However, from the mid-twentieth century the nurture side of this debate was in the ascendant, especially through the influence of a newly self-confident social sciences, and this came to be more or less the consensus view. Ideas about the biological character of social life followed a separate track and only occasionally, such as in the sociobiology debate of the 1970s discussed below (see p. 86), did they come into hailing (or more usually shouting) distance with the social sciences. More recently, with the upsurge of research in genetics, the nature–nurture pendulum seems to be swinging back in the direction of biology. However, in childhood studies the social view still tends to predominate with little dialogue across the divide that separates it from biology. This tendency was strengthened by the linguistic turn in the social theory and, associated with it, the emergence of social constructionism. The impact of these moves was felt in childhood studies through the new paradigm of childhood sociology. A central feature of this view was that, while the biological immaturity of children may be a fact, the real interest and future of childhood studies lies in the study of how cultures interpret such immaturity (Prout and James, 1990: 7).

In this chapter I want to reconsider this claim. The central argument that I will make is that rather than questioning the opposition between 'nature' and 'culture', the claim that childhood is a social construction reproduces it. It can be interpreted as a reverse discourse. The idea that childhood belongs to the domain of nature is met with the counter-claim that it belongs to culture. This maintains, endorses and arguably even strengthens the culture/nature opposition. In the short term there were benefits to be gained from this reverse discourse. It created what appear to be very strong defences against biological reductionism in the study of children. It allowed a free rein to the intellectual imagination, as long as it did not stray beyond the boundary of culture. It promoted the further exploration of the social, cultural and historical construction of childhood, opening up new areas of questioning and illuminating new aspects of children's lives. However, it did so at the cost of bracketing out or expelling biology, the body and even materiality as such from its accounts of childhood. In a longer-term perspective, especially if we are to move towards childhood studies as a distinct field, this is not a tenable or viable position.

I believe it is time to consider what sort of theoretical framework will allow childhood studies to develop as a multi-disciplinary or even inter-disciplinary field. In reconsidering this question I have come to think that childhood studies cannot base themselves upon a set of unexamined and problematic dualisms. The culture/nature division is one extremely, perhaps supremely, important instance of dualistic thinking. Just as a one-sided emphasis on biology means that much that is important about childhood is missed, so too does one-sidedly prioritizing culture over nature. Such reductionist tendencies disqualify themselves as starting points for the creation of childhood studies as a genuinely multi- or interdisciplinary field. In this chapter I will explore the possibility of finding a terrain on which it might be possible to go beyond the biology–culture opposition by exploring contemporary discussions in two topics: evolutionary perspectives on childhood and the sociology of the body.

Science and society

The aim of this chapter, then, is to move beyond the dualisms of nature and culture by examining how culture and nature can be seen as mutually constitutive. The basics of this position were set out in the previous chapter in my exposition of Latour's (1993) account of how modernity separated nature and culture (its work of purification) and simultaneously hybridized them in its intensive and accelerating production of technologies, artefacts and machines (its work of mediation). However, Latour's approach also encompasses and expresses a way of looking at the relationship between science and society. This is a topic of some importance to the study of childhood because it raises important questions about what it means for scientists to engage in the study of nature and the relationship between this endeavour and society/culture.

Early efforts to look at this relationship, called the 'weak programme' of science studies and exemplified by the writings of Robert Merton, accepted the claim of the natural sciences to stand outside social and cultural life and to be engaged in the production of universal, culture-free truths. Social influences were seen to enter this process only when science became ideologically distorted. The pressure put on scientists to conform to the political tenets of Stalinism and Nazism would be an example of this. However, the weak programme became an untenable position when social studies of 'good science', work that could not be accused of being overtly distorted by ideology, were also shown to be influenced by the social conditions in which they took place.

Although not determined by these in any simple way, it became clear that all science, whether good, bad or indifferent, is 'shaped' by the social and historical circumstances of its time. This is the so-called 'strong programme' of science studies, which is based on the overarching condition of scientific work – that it is a human activity. It cannot vault itself out of this predicament by pretending that language is transparent, that thinking can only be divided into error and truth, or that misunderstanding only arises from local prejudice. Science takes place in organizations, like laboratories, which are every bit as 'social' as institutions such as schools, families and factories. It involves rivalries, contestation and the making and breaking of reputations that on close examination turn out to be not only conducted through rational means (see, for example, Mackenzie and Wajcman, 1985; Pickering, 1992). Above all, science involves representing nature in various ways. The discourse, concepts and vocabulary available to scientists are historically and socially located and they shape what is thinkable and sayable at a given time and place. Representation, in language and by other means, is a form of mediation. Mediations are never just transparent, they also add to and take away from that being represented. They are slippery and create effects not always intended or even apparent to those who do the representing.

So science does not simply reflect nature, it also constructs it (for a general philosophical discussion of such a position, see Rorty, 1981). Sometimes these constructions are obviously ideological, as in the examples of Stalinism and Nazism. However, most of the time they are more deeply encoded and less visible, drawing on the largely unquestioned beliefs within the horizon of a culture and a historical period. Furthermore, although nature is understood through representations, it is not equally amenable to all representations of itself. It resists some attempts at translation more than others, an experience central to the craft of science, such that there is a reciprocal relationship between science and nature. There is, therefore, always a dual figure in science: nature and representations of nature. What is more, this applies fully to the other side of the modern opposition between nature and culture. We thus have a four-cornered set of relationships in which nature, representations of nature, culture and representations of culture are all mutually implicated.

Each of these is 'real' and each has effects. They are all complexly related to each other. The ramifications of each one reaches into the others in ways that cannot always be fully unpicked. How, for example, could one say that representations of nature do not enter into culture? Watch TV for an evening and see how much scientific imagery is used. A few decades ago, for example, very few people talked about humans as 'programmed' to think in particular ways (see also Chapter 5). Computer science has put this metaphor into culture and it now forms a common idiom of everyday speech. Or how could one claim that culture does not affect nature in the face of global warming, fish populations in decline, the pollution of waterways and genetic engineering?

This understanding of how science works can also be exemplified by the writings of Donna Haraway (1990, 1991), especially those published in her remarkable books *Primate Visions* and *Simians, Cyborgs and Women*. In these, Haraway, who trained as a biologist but turned to the history of science later in her life, examines the work of primatologists. What is notable about Haraway's writing is that she makes a critical analysis of science without being critical of science per se. Her work is not animated by the fear of science, although she is clear that there are sometimes things to be feared, or by hostility to it. On the contrary, she readily concedes that work on primates has produced some of the best science of the twentieth century and it has greatly increased our understanding of animal behaviour and human evolution. Its stories are developed in critical debate and tested against the best evidence that is available. Nevertheless, the narratives it weaves are deeply infused with a view of the world coherent with contemporary capitalist economics and patriarchal practices.

The legacy of the sociobiology episode

Latour and Haraway's idea presents a promising way to approach the complex entanglements of nature and culture. However, reconstituting the ground on which biology and culture can be understood differently, as not necessarily oppositional, is not an easy task. There is no area of discussion in the social sciences more contentious or rancorous than that about the role of biology in social and cultural life. The history of attempts to apply biological thinking to social life over the last one-and-a-half centuries has provided many good reasons for distrusting the entire enterprise. Although the dominant reference point for this debate in recent times is the furore surrounding E.O. Wilson's (1980) book *Sociobiology*, first published in 1975, efforts to apply biological ideas, particularly evolutionary ideas, to human behaviour are longstanding. The self-serving teleologies of nineteenth- and early-twentieth-century Social Darwinism, in which race and class prejudice were given full rein to the more recent vulgarized ethnology of Morris's (1969) *The Naked Ape,* stand as stark warnings. Such ideas can rightly be dismissed as a distortion of Darwinian and modern evolutionist thinking. They base themselves, for example, on a progressive and linear idea of evolution that categorizes so-called 'lower' and 'higher' forms. This idea is in fact quite foreign to Darwinian thinking, which, certainly in its contemporary form, sees evolution as an open-ended and non-hierarchical process. Evolutionary biology does not endow evolution with a goal or direction towards which it is heading or for which it is striving. It does not provide a standard against which the 'superiority' of a species or an individual can be judged. Similarly, ethnological attempts, such as those of Konrad Lorenz (1970) to understand human behaviour through the concept of 'instinct', have utterly foundered because of their scientific inexactitude, their patent commission of the naturalistic fallacy, i.e. their effort to justify what is acceptable because it is 'natural', and their positing of a straight line between biology and social behaviour.

It was, however, against this historical background that E.O. Wilson catapulted his musings about the biological basis of social behaviour. Wilson's central claims about this are made in the final chapter of *Sociobiology.* As Laland and Brown (2002) point out, the vast majority of this book consists of a discussion of animal behaviour. Only in the last chapter did he turn his attention to human society, where he claimed that, while cultures vary and individuals do have a certain amount of choice about their behaviour, the human genetic endowment means that they are likely to think more strongly in some directions than others. Genes, he declared, hold culture on a leash and this means that all human cultures will converge towards certain predisposed traits. Such traits include a division of labour between the sexes, bonding between kin, suspicion of strangers and overall male dominance. Explanations for these were then devised which purported to show that these were evolved adaptations, inherent to the human species, forming in a sense our 'human nature'.

One can readily appreciate how provocative these claims were, especially in the radical political environment of the 1970s. His critics leapt upon these claims with much fervour. They suggested that they were an attempt to reinvigorate arguments of the Social Darwinist type, masking right-wing politics with a claim to scientific legitimacy and promoting racism, sexism and class prejudice. In some ways these political aspects overwhelmed the debate such that each side caricatured the other. The oppositional dichotomies stacked up so that to be 'left wing' was to believe in nurture and to be 'right wing' was to believe in nature. Interestingly, 30 years later, after a lot of social and political water has flowed under the bridge, we are beginning to see a looser alignment of political and scientific beliefs.

For example, a left-wing version of the 'nature story' is beginning to be elaborated. Richard Wilkinson (2000) argues that human societies evolved in a way that made equality and cooperation adaptive survival. Humans, it is suggested, are adapted for equality and it is the breach of this in the increasingly unequal societies of the capitalist world that best explains patterns of health inequality. Inequality, it is argued, makes us ill because it runs against our nature. However, such a position (whatever one makes of it) was not widely available in the heated political context within which sociobiology was first discussed.

In fact the political and the scientific elements of the sociobiology debate were closely intertwined. Since the Second World War the preference for a nurture rather than nature view of human development had gained ground, becoming in many ways the social science orthodoxy. This was often deployed in arguments for maintaining and expanding the welfare state or increasing sexual equality. It was highly challenging, therefore, for a counterblast supporting the hereditarian view to be so starkly proclaimed. However, the critics, whatever their political persuasions, were also on firm ground when they challenged the scientific logic of 1970s sociobiology. In particular they were right to point out that, for all their scientific language, sociobiologist hypotheses were little more than *post hoc* stories about human behavioural attributes. The arch critic (and biologist) Steven Rose, for example, wrote that all one must do to be a sociobiologist is: 'predicate a genetically determined contrast in the past and then use some imagination, in a Darwinian version of Kipling's *Just So Stories*' (Rose *et al.*, 1984: 258).

Then, as now, most social scientists are trained to believe that what makes their disciplines possible is the separate ontological status of nature and culture. Although this idea is weakening, for example through the realization that social life cannot be separated from the ecological processes of the planet, it still holds enormous sway. Many hang on to it as tenaciously as the religious opponents of Darwinism do to their inability to believe that humans evolved from apes. As I discussed in Chapter 3 the separation of nature and culture is one of the characteristics of modernist thinking. Given these beliefs (and, to be sure, their equivalent, mirror image ones among the natural scientists) it is hardly surprising that the ideas of sociobiology met with a sceptical reception among social scientists. That this scepticism became downright hostility is explained largely by the unconvincing and extremely careless way in which Wilson extended his ideas from non-human to human animals. The chapters that deal with animal behaviour are widely regarded as an important, even landmark, contribution to that field. The chapter concerned with human sociobiology is highly speculative and extraordinarily naive and insensitive about social and political issues (such as gender inequality or homosexuality). Furthermore, and an unfortunate general trait amongst biologists writing about social issues even today, it is unreflexive and careless about the language it uses. It gives little consideration to what most scholars of the social and cultural are trained to give much attention: the ways in which the representation of something can affect, indeed partially construct, what it is.

However, the sociobiology episode took place almost 30 years ago. In itself it generated very little that was useful in unpicking the connections between biology and society, except perhaps the need to do better. Its legacy was to increase the polarization of the biological and social sciences. Even in the 1970s, however, the alignment of the debate was not simple or straight-forward. The leading and most indefatigable opponents of Wilson's ideas were not necessarily social scientists. Biologists such as Rose and Lewontin were trenchant critics and many other evolutionary biologists were, and are, cautious about simplistic applications of evolutionary biology to human affairs. However, one would hardly know this if one were guided only by the hostility with which most sociologists greet any suggestion of a biologi-cal component to human social life. Still less would one know that over the last three decades evolutionary biologists have moved a long way in recognizing that culture plays a large and even partially independent role in human affairs.

It has taken a quarter of a century to reach a point where some more productive dialogue between biology and the social sciences can at least be envisaged. The ground for this debate has emerged through the separate work of biologists and social scientists. In general terms this has come about because the oppositions that dominated modernist thinking have been weakened – in the way signalled by Haraway at the head of this chapter. Partly because of this work the boundaries between living and non-living entities, between animal and human, human and non-human and between nature and culture have become less stable and more blurred.

Contemporary social biology

Evolutionary biology remains a complex, disparate field, riven by internal conflicts (see Brown, 2000, for a readable introduction). However, partic-ularly when it has focused its attention on the human species, it has made an important contribution to these destabilizations. In my view the most important contributions have come from those prepared to rethink the assumptions of earlier sociobiology and address the points made by its critics in a serious and sustained way. The idea that culture could be bracketed out of the picture, while allotting biology most of the explanatory power for human social behaviour, has been largely revised, if not abandoned, by many coming from the sociobiology tradition. Of course this is not to say that the ideas and formulations now discussed by biologists do not display some of the same problems of earlier sociobiology.

According to Laland and Brown (2002) four main trends can be found in current evolutionary biology: human behavioural ecology; evolutionary psychology; memetics; and gene–culture co-evolution. I do not have space, nor am I equipped, to adjudicate on the technical disputes between their various proponents and critics. Instead I will attempt only to convey a flavour of each by indicating the main direction of thinking, arranging them roughly in terms of their distance from earlier sociobiological ideas:

(a) Human behavioural ecology sets out to examine the relationship between environmental ecology and behavioural/cultural variability within and between human populations. In particular it is concerned to look at whether measured human behaviour accords with what would seem to be the optimal strategies predicted by evolutionary models, focusing on topics such as foraging strategies among hunter-gatherers and the trade-off between the number and quality of children born and reared (see, for example, Bogerhoff Mulder, 1998). The tendency is to view stable cultural practices as adaptive to and evoked by the ecology within which a group lives (thus rather underestimating the possibility of maladaptive behaviours persisting). It has remained very much a minority approach among anthropologists, in part because anthropologists usually see culture as a more or less autonomous entity and partly because the link between ecology and culture has proved to be a highly mediated process in which it is not possible to make very clear distinctions between natural and cultural components.

(b) Evolutionary psychology (see, for example, Buss, 1999) argues that human behaviour is not adaptive to contemporary circumstances but that human psychological mechanisms are adaptations which evolved to suit the needs of the past, specifically to the needs of human hunter-gatherer ancestors two million or so years ago (known as the EEA or 'environment of evolutionary adaptedness'). Consequently evolutionary psychologists do not focus on human behaviour as such but on the psychological mechanisms (such as a 'module' for mate choice, see Buss, 1994) that are said to underlie them. Critics (Laland and Brown, 2002) correctly claim that this is a speculative field ripe for the speculative 'Just So' stories to which 1970s sociobiology was so prone, as well as being based on dubious assumptions about the modular functionality of the mind. From a social science perspective evolutionary psychology is particularly naive about culture, seeing it merely as an aggregate effect of individual psychological mechanisms.

(c) Memetics is a more radical approach resulting from the evolutionary biologist Richard Dawkins's dissatisfaction with sociobiological explanations of human behaviour (Dawkins, 1976). In response to the criticism that culture is not explicable in biological terms he proposes that culture itself is subject to evolutionary processes. Of course ideas of cultural evolutionism have a largely discredited reputation in anthropology, where they are associated with the idea of progress from lower to higher stages of human civilization. Dawkins, however, does not make such a teleological argument. Instead he suggests that the gene, for Dawkins (though not, as we will see, for all biologists) the basic unit of biological replication, has a counterpart in the 'meme', which he claims as the basic unit of cultural replication. In this definition, a meme is a complex of ideas and beliefs such as faith in a god, a political cause or, indeed, scientific reason. He makes no claim about the content and direction but only the process of meme evolution. It possesses key characteristics that parallel biological evolution, making biological evolution a specific case of a more general process at work in the universe. Memes are transmitted through generations (and in this sense are inherited); there is a great variety of them at any one time; and they are subject to differential, context-related fitness pressures. However, Dawkins argues that memes may replicate in a way more autonomous than that encountered in the case of the gene. In effect he argues that a cultural formation may spread rapidly simply because it is very good at replicating itself. These claims might almost be a tongue-in-cheek riposte to social scientists who make inflated claims for the separation of culture from nature, for here culture, except at the deep level of processual homology, is given a highly autonomous role.

(d) The basic idea of gene–culture co-evolution is that humans inherit both genes and culture (Lumsden and Wilson, 1981). It attempts to simultaneously handle both biology and culture, arguing that evolutionary processes reorganized the human brain to acquire, store and use cultural information. Once this evolutionary milestone had occurred it gave humans great adaptive flexibility and the possibility of great cultural diversity. The interaction of genes and culture thus produces new possibilities. For example, genetic inheritance may influence which aspects of culture an individual is predisposed to learn. At the same time weak genetic biases can be culturally amplified or diminished in ways that give them greater or lesser social weight and influence. Like memetics, gene–culture evolution places a great emphasis on social learning. Partly in consequence of this it is explicitly non-adaptionist. Unlike earlier theories of sociobiology (and human behavioural ecology and aspects of evolutionary psychology) gene–culture co-evolution does not concern itself solely with genetic and/or cultural characteristics that appear to be adaptive. On the contrary it quite clearly allows for the possibility that cultural traits will arise and flourish even when they are not adaptive to the environment. For example, gene–culture co-evolution studies have suggested that, contrary to the usual assumption, dairy farming developed first and created selection pressures that led to the genetic basis for lactose absorption becoming more common (Holden and Mace, 1997).

In reviewing these four approaches Laland and Brown hold out the prospect of a rapprochement between the 'nature' view of the biological sciences and the 'culture' view of the social sciences:

Advocates of gene–culture co-evolution share with memeticists and the vast majority of social scientists the view that what makes culture different from other aspects of the environment is the knowledge passed between individuals. Culture is transmitted and inherited in an endless chain, frequently adapted and modified to produce cumulative evolutionary change. This infectious, information-based property is what allows culture to change rapidly, to propagate a novel behaviour through a population, to modify the selection pressures acting on genes, and to exert such a powerful influence on our behavioural development.

(Laland and Brown, 2002: 249)

This is clearly a step forward from the entrenched and polemical positions of the sociobiology war of the 1970s, and the possibility of moving beyond its simplicities is surely to be welcomed. However, for all the lucidity and level-headedness of their account, Laland and Brown underestimate at least four problems. First, they retain faith in science as a neutral, objective and fact-producing process. Their belief is that science, if stripped of ideological deformations such as the political undertow of the sociobiology debate, can 'chip away' at problems until they are solved. They seem unaware of more contemporary understandings of how 'science' and 'culture' are reciprocally constitutive. As already noted above, a writer such as Haraway (1991) does not argue that current sociobiology is simply an ideological mask for social interests. Rather she shows how evolutionary biology shares, draws on and contributes culture-bound metaphors for speaking its subject matter. Second, they defend what they see as the strength of reductionism as the main method of scientific enquiry and express themselves as impatient with holistic thinking. This is, I think, mistaken for although holism can lapse into obscurantism (and even mysticism) the ideas of complexity theory, which are a form of holism, have an important place in scientific thinking (see Chapter 3 and pp. 93–4). Third, as the above quotation shows, they are content with a view of culture and nature that remains dualistic. Memetics and gene–culture theories have an *interactive* view of culture and nature that assumes their fundamental separateness. Fourth, there is a strong tendency to methodological individualism in their account and in the approaches of the scientists whom they see as pointing the way forward. This is apparent, for example, in the assumption that cultural transmission takes place through the learning processes of individual minds or that culture is simply an aggregate of individual behaviour. As a result the collective features of human societies, whether these be social institutions or material artefacts that play a crucial role in ordering social life and stabilizing culture, are played down.

However, there are accounts of the relationship between culture and biology that do address these questions. It was noted above that many of the harshest critics of 1970s sociobiology came from biologists themselves. The eminent biologist Richard Lewontin, for example, was and remains a critic of sociobiology while being simultaneously concerned to understand human society and culture from a materialist, and therefore partially biological, perspective. Lewontin (2000) has a view of the social that is much more sophisticated than the methodological individualism that pervades much writing in this field. Developing a more or less Marxist view of social life he is clear that social phenomena are collective and relational; they are more than the outcome of the activities of ontologically prior individuals. He is clear that science takes place in and is shaped by social conditions. In particular, he argues that the direction of genetic studies is marked by capitalist interests. More than this, however, he is clear that science is caught up in the very language it employs. He argues, for example, that the metaphor of 'development' constructs phenomena as if they unfolded from within, producing something that already exists – like the idea that human development is an expression of genes, which form a kind of blueprint of the individual. Lewontin rather sees a network of reciprocal relationships that come about over time but in non-teleological ways. 'Evolution' he says 'is not an unfolding but an historically contingent wandering pathway through the space of possibilities' (2000: 88). The development of an individual organism is the result of both genetic make-up and the environment – but the whole process is folded into an environment that is already partially produced by organisms and their histories:

> The relations of genes, organisms, and environments are reciprocal relations in which all three elements are both causes and effects. Genes and environments are both causes of organisms, which are, in turn, causes of environments, so that genes become causes of environments as mediated by the organisms.
>
> (2000: 100–1)

The implication of this is that genes, organisms and environments cannot be meaningfully studied as if they were separate entities because their histories are already implicated with each other.

Lewontin is just one example of applying what Gray (1992) and Oyama (1985) call 'developmental systems' to evolutionary processes. Oyama, discussing the issue in terms of information transmission in genetic and evolutionary processes, spells out the implications of this approach very clearly:

> [T]he influences and constraints on (a system's) responsiveness are a function of both the presenting stimulus and the results of past selections, responses, and integrations, and that organisms organize their surroundings even as they are organized by them. This being the case, developmental pathways are not set in any substantive way either by the genome or by the environment, regardless of the normality or relative probability of the pathway itself.
>
> (Oyama, 1985: 169)

Such a system can be considered very similar to the complex systems discussed in Chapter 3. Rather than thinking of the biological and the social as two different kinds of entity that are then brought into interaction, this approach starts with the idea of a system made of multiple interconnections. Like all complex systems these contain different levels: the molecular; the cellular; the organism; the society. Reciprocal relations take place between all these different levels and the system (and its various levels and regions) develops (non-teleologically) over time. Thus an individual organism, or even a whole species over an evolutionary temporal scale, though occupying different levels or regions of the whole, can be thought of in the same terms:

> [T]he effects of both genetic and environmental differences are contingent on the context in which they occur ... The impact of an environmental factor will vary depending on the developmental state of the organism and, reciprocally, the effect of a gene being activated will depend on the state of the rest of the developmental system ... The reciprocal and temporal contingency of developmental causation not the simple addition of a genetic and an environmental vector ... causation must therefore be conceptualised in system rather than vector terms.
>
> (Gray, 1992: 175–6)

In Chapter 3, I set out a way of adapting Bronfenbrenner's idea of linking the individual child to the macro social system via a meso level that mediates this relationship. However, I argued that it makes more sense to see the levels not as independently constituted, pre-given 'containers' but as contingently constructed through the networks and flows that traverse them, flows that consist of the people, texts and things. This image can now also be applied to the biological, and indeed chemico-physical, level that includes molecules, genes, the physical environment and living organisms. All these together, and according to the history of the system, shape the developmental pathway.

The evolution of juvenility in animal species

Before returning to some of these themes in relation to the development of childhood bodies, I want to consider what biology, especially evolutionary biology, has to say that is of more direct interest to childhood studies. In fact, irrespective of its conceptualization in terms of a complex system, there is a lot that is pertinent to the study of childhood, although the word 'childhood' is rarely used (but see Bogin, 1998, and below). The term used by biologists is rather 'juvenility' (Pereira, 2002). This is more than a merely semantic difference. 'Juvenility' refers to a widespread phenomenon amongst animals in which an individual is sexually immature but able to survive the absence of parental care (because it is no longer dependent on this care for its survival). Such periods of juvenility are in fact quite common and evolutionary biologists have long been interested in why some species have a juvenile stage while others do not. Such juvenile stages appear across all the main animal taxa (including amphibians, reptiles, fishes, birds and mammals). Juvenility is not restricted by the size of the species and it occurs in species with a huge variety of modes of existence. The case of the Pacific salmon, which spend two or three years feeding at sea before starting their epic journey to reproduce, and die, in their fresh-water spawning grounds, is well known. The periodic cicadas, that entertain or enrage with their diurnal chirruping, can spend 17 years feeding underground before emerging ready to mate. Female turtles can take up to 30 years to reach sexual maturity.

From an evolutionary perspective the delay in reproductive capacity that juvenility involves seems, at first sight, very puzzling. Natural selection would seem to favour the earliest possible reproduction within the life history of an animal. Early reproduction would therefore seem to provide the best chance of an animal species perpetuating itself. The life span of all animals is limited by predation and disease and it would seem that the sooner an individual is physiologically capable of reproduction then the better would be its chances of actually producing offspring. Early reproductive capacity extends the lifetime possibility of reproductive success, it reduces the length of a generation and so increases the chance of geometric population growth. All of this would seem to mitigate against extended juvenility.

Why, then, should a species benefit from delaying maturation? In trying to answer this question evolutionary biologists have revealed the wonderful complexity of biological processes and their intricate imbrication with both ecology and sociality. The general framework of their research is to consider the factors that maximize reproductive potential across the *whole life span* of an individual. Such factors include species-specific ones such as the duration of incubation and gestation, offspring size and number as well as ecological ones such as seasonality and the abundance of food. It is argued that how resources are allocated to growth, maintenance and reproduction, *and at what stage in the life history of a species*, is crucial to the emergence of strategies that maximize reproductive potential. The life history of a species thus itself becomes the object of evolutionary processes. In a given ecological niche a particular life-history pattern, involving a longer or shorter, or even absent, period of juvenility will tend to be selected because it increases the survival of the organism. The overall picture is summarized by Pereira (2002: 26):

> The general function of animal juvenility is modulation of growth and the onset of reproduction. In many cases it functions to maximize the rate and/or extend the duration of growth, therefore allowing it to

escape the period during which small size renders it particularly vulner-able to predation and virtually ineligible to compete for reproductive opportunity . . . Conversely, when small size entails little cost or when large size is penalised by the environment, juvenility often is abbrevi-ated or does not occur in a life history. Juvenility is also diminished when adult size can be attained by or soon after the exhaustion of parental provision, as in many birds and mammals, or when early reproductive effort does not compromise further growth.

Juvenility can thus be seen as a result of a set of complex evolutionary trade-offs. Evolutionary biologists are far from fully understanding how these mechanisms work but they can point to some of the factors and processes involved. For instance, greater hardness (such as having or devel-oping a shell, like a turtle) or larger size at birth can increase survivability and this is often associated with delay in the capacity to reproduce. Conversely, species that produce small and vulnerable young often have accelerated periods of growth in the first part of their life. Sexual selection can also play a role. When mating is monopolized by a few large, domi-nant males, early reproductive maturity runs the risk of injury and death from intrasexual aggression. This correlation can, however, also be affected by ecological factors (Warner, 1984), so that evolutionary pressure for or against juvenility must also be understood in the context of the interplay between a species and its environment. Some species seem to respond to their environment by adapting their pattern of development and it has been suggested that, even in non-mammals, social factors, deriving from the collective, group life of a species, can affect the presence of extended juven-ility. Complex mathematical models comparing how life-history variables correlate within and across taxa have been developed in order to explore these processes. However, the factors involved have to be understood as dynamic and non-linear. As Pereira (2002: 20) puts it: 'Shifts in the timing of maturation rarely leave other life-history traits unaffected.'

Many, though not all, species of mammals have an extended juvenile period. Conventionally, evolutionary biology has offered two competing explanations for this trend. The first suggests that the age of first repro-duction can be explained in terms of the final size of a species and constraints (such as effects of the seasons) on growth rates. The second approach prior-itizes demographic factors. Crudely stated this suggests that species with high rates of mortality will have early ages of reproduction. Pagel and Harvey (2002) have explored these using comparative data across species. Although there are major gaps in its explanatory power, they conclude that body size (and constraints on growth rates) plays the most obvious and important role in extending mammalian juvenility. However, they go on to suggest that important selective advantages accrue when individuals use their extended juvenile period to develop skills that aid their survivability:

Behaviours such as play and mock-hunting, or the learning of social skills may evolve because of the juvenile period and even reinforce it. Their influence may be on adult mortality rate, fecundity, or juvenile survivorship. Where such influences are important, we expect age at maturity to be delayed even further than the point set by selection acting, via adult mortality rates, on adult body size . . . Much of the variation that remains after controlling for size is probably attributable to the skills and knowledge that juveniles acquire during their apprenticeship to become adults.

(Pagel and Harvey, 2002: 37)

Earlier it was noted that life-history trajectory has to be understood in relation to the environment. Various regulatory feedback mechanisms can occur as animals sense their environment and change in response to it. In non-mammals this may be thought to take place through non-cognitive mechanisms. However, in mammals (and, as we shall see, especially primates) learning in its cognitive sense seems to play a similar, if rather more complex, role. Social learning, play and trial-and-error practices can develop as an evolutionary strategy alongside extended juvenility.

However, it is an error to suppose that play and learning function only to produce adults who are better fitted to survive. This may be part of the picture but the overall position of contemporary biologists is interestingly parallel to that adopted by social scientists in relation to human children. As Rubenstein (2002: 56) argues:

play may indeed serve to enhance social and cognitive skills and to develop motor proficiency . . . But not because play prepares a juvenile to become a better adult, but because the benefits of play help to make a better juvenile, one that is competent presently and will increase its chances of surviving, not necessarily one that will be better able to cope with the unique problems that beset adults.

Primates and humans

So far, this discussion of juvenility has concerned non-human animals. However, what inspires biological thinking in relation to social life is the basic Darwinian insight that the human species also emerged through an evolutionary process that both links it to the animal kingdom and marks its specific characteristics. As we have seen, until recently much of the biological thinking about this has been speculative and has stressed the continuities between biology and human behaviour rather than acknowledging the crucial role that culture plays in the shaping of human societies. However, few would deny the importance of the suggestion, made by Darwin over a century ago, that the similarities between humans and the modern African apes points to their sharing a common ancestor. Studies of the fossil record since then and, more recently, of human and ape DNA have confirmed that this does indeed seem to be the case. The story that scholars of evolution tell us is an unfolding and changing one. At the present time the best interpretation of the evidence suggests that the climate changed in Africa some six million years ago, transforming the dense forest, within which a wide variety of ape species thrived, into open woodland. This had a drastic impact on many ape species, bringing about extinctions and new adaptations. The survivor of this period of transformation was the common ancestor of the modern apes and the modern humans.

The most iconic piece of evidence is 'Lucy', the ape skeleton fossil found by the paleoanthropologist Don Johansen at the Ethiopian end of the African Rift Valley in 1974. Although it is contested how efficient she was at it, Lucy was undoubtedly a bipedal ape. The anatomy of her foot and other evidence show that she had the capacity to walk upright. Many further remains of such bipedal apes, populating the African Rift Valley about three-and-a-half million years ago, have been found. The evolutionary approach, however, is not teleological. It does not suggest that bipedalism occurred in order to allow the development of hands that were free for the food gathering and carrying, making of gestures or using tools that were to become human specialities. Bipedalism must have had a survival value in its own terms. But whatever this was it set the proto-hominids apart from the apes (who, though they can adopt a bipedal stance, do not do so habitually and are not anatomically adapted for it). The exact sequence of the transition from bipedal ape to human is highly contested. Nevertheless it seems that by about one-and-a-half million years ago a distinct species had emerged, *Homo erectus*, thought by some to be just one of fifteen different human species that had existed and become extinct in the period between one and three million years ago. *Homo erectus* had a larger body size than other hominids and a larger brain too. It was a highly successful species that gradually migrated out of Africa and populated the rest of the globe.

One of the main products of the mediation between nature and culture is technology and all the vast array of material artefacts involved in human life. These, as already suggested in Chapter 1, play an important (though not simply determinant) part in contemporary childhood and its trajectories of change. Modern primate studies, however, are breaking down any very distinct boundary between humans and our nearest biological relatives among the primates. While human culture is diverse and prolific, primatologists argue that it can also be said to exist among chimpanzees. Tool use in itself is not a mark of culture but among chimpanzees it has been shown that creative innovations in tool use can be seen. Differences in tool use among groups of chimpanzees cannot be explained as ecological adaptations because they do not merely reflect the differential availability of materials. Furthermore, tool use and the deployment of different methods (for example, of gathering ants as a food source) can be shown to be socially learnt.

Similarly, while humans have a very well-developed capacity for language, this is also found to a degree among chimpanzees. Here is a summary of current primatological studies:

> Chimpanzees lack the ability to make complex, abstract representations of word meanings; their ability to do this is at the level of a two-and-a-half-year-old child. They can comprehend and produce syntactical structures. In the realm of cognition they can comprehend things about the state of mind of others, but not to the same degree as human children. They can imitate, but not well, or perhaps only emulate. And they have concepts of number sequences, sums and fractions at the level of a three-year-old child.
>
> (Stanford, 2001: 161)

However, Stanford goes on to argue that attempts to teach chimpanzees human language are far less important than the effort to understand communication between chimps themselves. This is known to happen but at the moment is hardly understood at all. Be that as it may, when confronted with such findings it becomes increasingly difficult to maintain that there is a very sharp line between humans and at least some of the primates. Perhaps, as Gibson (1993: 8) remarks, there has been:

> a tendency to define tool-making, symbolism, syntax, culture and other capacities as all-or-nothing phenomena which an animal either does or does not possess. Perhaps . . . it is time to abandon all-or-none definitions and think of complex behaviours as existing in various levels or degrees.

From this perspective, what is striking is the way that behaviours which in other animals exist in isolation or in rudimentary forms are among humans interactively generative, 'yielding a cultural product much greater than the sum of its individual parts' (Gibson, 1993: 136). Tool use among human ancestors can be inferred from the archaeological record up to two million years ago but in cultural symbolism it is well evidenced only during the last 40,000 years. The emergence of the human species involved the modification of the function of the hand and the mouth in a way that made possible (though not by design or intention) the use of tools and language. As Gibson notes:

> Quite apart from sharing similar neurological, cognitive, and structural substrates, language and tool-use may have mutual feedback and facilitative mechanisms . . . Many anthropologists have reiterated and expanded upon the potential interrelationships between the planning involved in tool-using and making endeavours and speech.
>
> (Gibson, 1993: 10)

The development of language is not a well understood evolutionary process. The fossil record suggests a slow, gradual development over hundreds of thousands of years and the archaeological record suggesting a much later development concentrated around the relatively more recent emergence of *Homo sapiens* (Lewin, 1993: 457–67). In either case speech is a means by which brain activity (memory, consciousness, thinking) can be externalized, shared, transmitted from one generation to the next and enter into social processes. In this respect speech has a counterpart in gesture and that gesture combined with tools creates techniques. One such technique was 'graphism', the making of pictorial representations, that creates the possibility of durable, material images that act as another means of social, including intergenerational, transmission. Furthermore, techniques and technologies (for a distinction, see Ingold, 1993) create 'extensions' to the human body that give it greater power, reach and effectivity, merging the human and the non-human in the construction of social life. As we saw in Chapter 1 and will revisit in Chapter 5, contemporary childhood is not comprehensible without considering these socio-technical dimensions.

Primate juvenility

As we have seen, primates are not unique in having an extended juvenile period. Nevertheless, primates do have a remarkably extended period of juvenility. In fact an extended period of immaturity is the most important marker of difference in life-history pattern between primates and other mammals. Primates also show a pattern of growth quite atypical for mammals. Non-primate mammals typically go through a period of rapid growth soon after birth. In contrast, growth in young primates slows down a few days or weeks after birth and this slow rate of growth persists until puberty, when there is a growth spurt associated with the renewed production of hypothalmic, pituitary and gonadal hormones. Bogin (1998), however, makes a case for believing that 'childhood' is an additional stage in the growth and development of an individual that is unique to the human species. Where apes have a sequence that includes 'infancy', 'juvenility' and 'adulthood', humans have 'inserted' the childhood stage (which he counts in age terms as between two and seven years) between infancy and juvenility. His argument rests on a number of differences, claimed as qualitative rather than quantitative, between the pattern of growth of primates and humans. For example, compared to apes human children's brains are relatively large. This is due to the fact that, unlike most primates, the brains of human children grow quickly before birth and continue to grow after birth. Human brains are also organized differently in ways associated with possession of speech and handedness. This is an interesting idea that links childhood with an evolutionary strategy linked to culture and that therefore depends for its success on intensified parental (and other adult?) socialization. However, though interesting it remains somewhat speculative.

Whether or not childhood is a distinct phase or a version of juvenility, and despite the importance of extended juvenility among primates, only a small proportion of the research effort that has gone into primates has been concerned with juveniles. Primatologists interested in juveniles complain long and hard about this fact. For example, two of the world's leading authorities on the subject write that:

> after 35 years of modern research on primate behaviour and ecology, the juvenile period remains the most neglected phase of life histories . . . This situation is ironic because protracted development, including extended juvenility or delayed sexual maturation, is the life history feature that best distinguishes the order Primates among the mammals.
> (Perreira and Fairbanks, 2002: 3)

Here is something else that biology and sociology share. Sociologists of childhood have also had to overcome the resistance of their own adult-centred discipline with a long history neglecting children. Pereira and Fairbanks have to address and rebut very similar assumptions among prima-tologists that (adult-centric) sociologists make about human children. They are, for example, at pains to show that juvenile primates are not innocent. 'Immatures' they write 'readily assimilate rules for behaviour, and at times they appear equally adept at operating and appearing to operate them' (Perreira and Fairbanks, 2002: 4). Neither are juvenile primates 'incomplete'. They are, it is argued, best thought of as 'different'. Different because they are specialized for using their time wisely until the point that they are able to reproduce. They are also energetic and curious. And among the greatest dangers they face is the fact that they must live in a world that is dominated by adults.

Biologists long ago recognized that there is a general relationship between the number of offspring, their survival and the intensity of parental care. Primates seem to have evolved a survival strategy based on producing a small number of young who are given a high level of support and care by parents. There is much debate among evolutionary biologists about the conditions that could give rise to this as an evolutionary pathway. A basic feature of this seems to be that primate pathways are invested in the development of a large brain. The hypothesis is that the heightened risks of predation that slow somatic growth implies are outweighed by the cognitive and behavioural advantages that this brings, especially when a heightened level of care by parents and other social allies is taken into account. This social context of development is emerging as a more and more important factor in understanding primate evolution. The development of a large brain is linked to social learning and play which seem to occupy an especially important role in primate development. However, play is a costly business and it can be a dangerous one too. Studies of non-primate mammals suggest that extended play is not an adaptive behaviour that increases survivability.

The picture in primates, however, is different. Play seems to occur in ways that shape neural pathways in an optimal way. The peaks of different types of play coincide with periods when brain development is most plastic. This seems to confer advantages both to the survival of the young and to their lifetime survival as adults (Janson and Van Schaik, 2002).

Many of these possible explanations await further exploration in future studies. However, it is likely that the overall evolutionary pathway taken by non-human primates (large complex brains, slow bodily growth, delayed reproduction, and long lives) took a further step in the case of human evolution. In the human case the amount and types of social care provided by parents and other adults are enhanced. The provision of protection, food, shelter and social learning to young humans allowed the primate evolutionary strategy to be intensified. The result was a period of juvenility, which may be countable as a distinct stage, but is in any case more extended than in any other ape.

The body, childhood and society

One of the products of the evolution of humans is the specific character of the human body and the sequence of its growth and development in childhood (and, indeed, beyond). It is not surprising, therefore, to find that, given the opposition between culture and nature in modernist thought, the body has been absent from much social theory, especially that associated with sociology. Although there was a substantial tradition within anthropology that was interested in the human body as a resource and product of social processes, this tradition became rather occluded in the post-Second World War environment of the social sciences. It was overtaken and overshadowed by a focus on social structure (conceived in terms of class, gender and race), social interaction (conceived largely as a symbolic process) and culture (also thought of in symbolic and textual terms). However, this began to change in sociology during the 1980s when there was a re-discovery of the body as a topic of social theory and an upsurge in interest in the body as a topic of social enquiry. This work involved the revisiting of earlier anthropological work but was also strongly influenced by the linguistic turn in social theory. The result of this thinking was that outlined by Turner (1984, 1992). His central conclusion was that there was a tendency for sociological work to divide between what he termed 'foundationalist' and 'anti-foundationalist' approaches. While Turner argued that both approaches are inadequate in themselves and that some theoretical synthesis or transcendence was required, his characterizations make a useful starting point for exploring the issues at stake in this debate.

These two tendencies mirror the general trend identified by Latour for the social sciences to draw nature and culture further and further apart – ending in their complete detachment in postmodern thinking. In this sense the foundationalists adhere to the historically earlier position of phenomenology. The body is considered as a real, but rather unproblem-matically pre-given material entity. Within this perspective social scientists are concerned with the many different frameworks of meaning in which the body is variously represented in human cultures. The body has meaning 'written on it'. At its most basic, foundationalists assume that there is some-thing constant (but perhaps changing) which functions independently of the social context within which it is found. In a sense this is the body that biol-ogists would recognize. The body (and its processes of change) form an entity which is experienced and lived. What is prioritized in this perspec-tive, therefore, is largely phenomenological. The task of sociologists is to document and analyse how the body is experienced and interpreted by different actors in different social and cultural contexts.

Anti-foundationalists, however, take a quite different point of view, one based on a social constructionist position. They are unwilling to make a distinction between the body and its representations (see Armstrong, 1983; and this volume, Chapter 2). In an extreme form anti-foundationalists might argue in an entirely idealist fashion: that there is no material body – only constructions or understandings of it. Less extreme, but also less consistent, is the view that even if the materiality of the body is conceded we only have access to it through discourse of various kinds. It is these discourses, or ways of representing the body, that structure and shape our experiences of it and the meanings we give to it. In this view, then, the task of social scientists is to analyse these representations and uncover the social processes through which they are made and have their effects.

The problem is that, as Turner argues, it is not possible to be simulta-neously and consistently foundationalist and anti-foundationalist – because each position is defined in opposition to the other. Turner's suggested way out of this problem is methodological eclecticism: that is to say he suggests accepting the intellectual legitimacy of both approaches, using each as and when it is appropriate and seeing them as in some way different but comple-mentary. While this allows empirical flexibility and diversity of approach, it is not theoretically coherent: different and irreconcilable assumptions are being made about the material character of the body. In taking up this point, Shilling suggests that Turner fails in his ambition to synthesize foundation-alist and anti-foundationalist approaches and argues (in effect though not quite in these terms) that this is because his method is additive rather than relational. Turner, he correctly observes, attempts to 'combine foundation-alist and anti-foundationalist frameworks without altering any of their basic parameters' (Shilling, 1993: 103). Consequently, Turner does not examine the *relationships* between the body in nature and the body in society.

Accordingly Shilling attempts to synthesize the two approaches and in so doing develops a position that is of great potential for studies of child-hood. The essence of his suggestion is that the human body is socially and biologically unfinished at birth. Over the life course, and childhood would seem to be a crucial stage, it changes through processes that are simultaneously biological and social. Drawing on a very wide range of social theory he suggests two basic elements of a framework. The first, that the mind–body relationship has to be seen in the wider context of the culture–nature relationship, is drawn from both anthropological and feminist analyses. Important among the former is the theory of symbol and metaphor developed by Lakoff and Johnson (1980). They argue that there is a close, but not one-to-one, relationship between mind and body as a result of the mind being located in and dependent on bodily mechanisms for the perception of the natural world. We exist, for example, in a world where gravity creates the phenomenon of motion as 'up' or 'down' and human thought incorporates, draws on and elaborates this phenomenon. Feminist writers have also, though to different degrees, pointed to irreducible biological differences between the sexes that shape experience differently for men and women. While some feminist analyses tend towards biological reductionism (often with an inversion of male claims to superiority), others look to an interaction between biological and social processes in which natural differences are transformed or distorted into social ones (Chernin, 1983; Orbach, 1986). In these accounts the body is not only shaped by social relations but also enters into their construction as both a resource and a constraint.

An equally important element of Shilling's approach is the suggestion that once we grant the body a biological/physical existence we can begin to see how it is worked on by society. Some of this work occurs through the symbolic and discursive practices highlighted by social constructionism – the body is represented and classified in various ways. However, many social practices are also material ones, for example diet, exercise and disciplinary regimes, and these concretely shape the body. For example, in the UK the prevalence of obesity among four- to twelve-year-olds in England doubled between 1984 and 1994 (Parliamentary Office of Science and Technology, 2003). The US shows a similar trend, with an estimated fifteen per cent of six- to nineteen-year-olds being judged overweight (National Center for Health Statistics, 2003). In fact, the proportion of overweight children is rising internationally (International Obesity Task Force, 2003) and the trend is not confined only to rich countries. These changes in body size and shape are too rapid to be explained by genetic causes and are taken to reflect changes in diet and physical activity. However, while these contemporary findings are fuelling efforts to change diet and exercise regimes, the link between the social circumstances of children and their bodily development is a long-standing finding of research (see Chapter 2). For example, the relationship between poverty, weight and physical growth is a feature of international comparisons (see, for example, Birch and Dye, 1970: 46–80, 177–220; UNICEF, 1996: 82–5).

So relationship between the body and society is reciprocal: society works on the body, just as the body works on society. As well as its evolutionary and genetic histories the body has a social one and because these are co-produced these histories become fused together. The theme of the body as socially and biologically unfinished promises to reconnect what social constructionism separated. It draws attention to how the body and society work on each other. This is, in fact, a theme that emerges in recent empirical research. For example, Christensen (2000) and Milburn (2000) show how children's bodies are the targets of parental practices, while Simpson (2000) describes how teachers attempt to regulate the appearance and time/space trajectories of their bodies in school. James (2000) revisits her earlier ethnography, re-emphasizing the active role of children but now placing this in temporal perspective, suggesting how children negotiate and re-negotiate identities. In the process of growing up, bodily changes create new possibilities; children cannot control bodily changes but through skilful handling can use them as flexible resources for translation into identity. Similarly Prendergast (2000) shows how girls manage bodily changes at menarche in home and school settings which render menstruation as a shameful secret. The multifaceted character of these practices, at one and the same time biological and social, can be contrasted with the analysis of children's bodies in a social constructionist account such as Armstrong's (1983, 1987; see also Chapter 2 of this volume). Enlightening though this account is of how medicine created categories of children, the body remains remarkably incorporeal. Armstrong's body is, in Terence Turner's terms, an 'anti-body', one which:

> has no flesh; . . . is begotten out of discourse by power . . . the desires that comprise its illusory subjectivity are themselves the predicates of external discourses rather than the products or metaphorical expressions of any internal life of its own.
>
> (Turner, 1994: 36)

Recent writers within the sociology of childhood do not neglect or underestimate how powerful discursive formations can be in shaping how children's bodies are perceived, understood, worked upon and produced. Christensen's (2000) account of the manner in which notions of children's essential vulnerability enter into adult understandings of even the most commonplace of accidents or mishaps in the school playground illustrates this well. However, as her account also implies, confining the attention only to representations of the body, and not examining the reciprocal relations between children and the body, is unsatisfactory (see also Christensen, 1999).

It is somewhat surprising that Shilling devotes so little attention to childhood. It would after all appear to be a time when work on and by the body is relatively intense. Childhood per se, however, appears in relation to only two of Shilling's substantive topics. The first is Elias's account of the 'civilizing process', that is the long-term historical trend towards individuals practising internalized control and restraint over forms of behaviour concerned with bodily functions such as eating, copulating and defecating. The second is Bourdieu's account of the transmission of class habitus. From the point of view of the sociology of childhood both Elias and Bourdieu are deficient, or at best ambiguous, in their assumptions about childhood socialization. Both seem to treat children as passively and gradually accreting or accumulating embodied dispositions in the transition to the full sociality of adulthood. There is little (or only equivocal) recognition of the possibility that children actively appropriate and transform as well as absorb. Nor is there a sense that childhood and growing up are full of reversals, transformations and inversions rather than being a progression to an ever-closer copy of adulthood. In short what is missing is a sense of children as beings as well as becomings, childhood as staged and children as active, creative performers (see also, for example, Bluebond-Langner *et al.*, 1991).

Several writers have recently shown how children are actively engaged in work on and with the body. Milburn (2000), for example, shows how middle-class children and parents translate, and thereby partially transform, official discourses of health into everyday practices. While adhering to the rhetoric of health promotion, officially sanctioned behaviour is also practically contested, subverted and renegotiated in families according to countervailing pressures and interests. This shows that, far from being docile in the face of officially distributed norms, children (as well as parents) are actively involved in negotiating their meaning and in resisting or modifying their implementation. Prendergast (2000) and Christensen (2000) illustrate how the body and society are inextricably woven together at particular moments of the life course. The former shows how the body is shaped by and is shaping of feminine identity as girls experience menarche. She examines how adolescent girls on the cusp of womanhood live a present which in its social and material arrangements emphasizes the shame and secrecy of menstruation. Through this they gaze into a future when their body is rendered problematic and at the same time are able to remember a childhood past when the relationship between gender and identity could be flexible and open. As she has pointed out:

> The issue of embodiment as a cultural process surfaces most poignantly at key points in the life cycle: the trajectory of the body is given symbolic and moral value: bodily forms are paradigmatic of social transition . . . Each stage requires that we adjust to and attend to our body, or that of others, in an appropriate and special way.
>
> (Prendergast, 1992: 1)

The possibility that childhood is created through, even perhaps requires, certain kinds of bodily performance is directly addressed by Christensen's work (2000 and 1999). She shows not only their creative activity but also that contemporary children inhabit a highly staged world – 'childhood' that is marked off from the rest of society. As such it stands in paradoxical relationship to the adult world and cannot be taken as an incomplete or faulty version of it. In her theoretical discussion Christensen raises important questions about 'vulnerability' as one of the central defining features of this contemporary childhood. Rather than accepting children's vulnerability as simply a fact of nature, she proposes the need for investigation into the components of this vulnerability. She suggests that while children, like many others, may at times be vulnerable, there is a push towards its use as a master identity for children. Ideologically children are separated from adults, rendered as objects of concern, help and intervention, and minimized in their capacity for dealing with their problems. At the same time their actual experiences, those that they experience as vulnerability, are not much listened to by adults. Children themselves, Christensen shows, are intensely interested in their own bodily experiences, describing children's 'body project' as a search for meanings and understandings constructed through a *bricolage* of bits and pieces of experience, and lay and biomedical categories.

Work of this kind shows how the notion of the body as socially and biologically unfinished might be worked through in relation to children – provided that children's interpretative activity as social beings is also appreciated. Children's bodies then appear in a variety of roles: in the construction of social relations, meanings and experiences between children themselves and with adults; as products of and resources for agency, action and interaction; and as sites for socialization through embodiment. By emphasizing the relationship of the body and society they begin to under- mine the notion that it is possible to understand social relations as if the body were able to be abstracted from them. In doing this they make an important move towards the hybrid character of social life as it applies to childhood.

Bio-technical-social translation

Treating the body as part of and not separate from social life has been an important step in creating the ground on which a more productive dialogue between the natural and the social sciences about childhood can take place. However, an account of childhood that includes only the terms biology and society misses the extremely important fact, discussed above in relation to the human evolutionary process, that human life also takes place through artefacts, technologies and machines of all kinds. Tool use is a strongly developed feature of the human species. Culture is not only symbolic but also material. This means moving beyond the relationship between body and society per se and locating this in the dense, networked heterogeneity that is social life. A highly pertinent example of this approach is found in the work of Bernard Place (2000). He shows how different approaches to the body might be integrated by looking at the processes surrounding the intensive combination of children's bodies with medical technologies. The ethnographic location he chose was the modern hospital, specifically a paediatric intensive care unit. He points out that in this particular location the human body is perforated, cannulated, intubated and catheterized before being connected to sets of technological artefacts which enable detailed examination of the functioning of the heart, kidneys, brain, lungs and other organs. Such artefacts generate sets of symbols (traces, numbers and images) which are manipulated by the doctors and nurses. In the process of connection to these artefacts the body is ordered, externalized and its boundary extended. The body becomes circumscribed by both corporeal (human) and non-corporeal (technological) elements, becoming in Place's term 'technomorphic'.

In this setting the nurses and doctors, as well as the parents and child patients, are concerned to maintain the integrity of the body. But what is the body in these circumstances? On the basis of his participant observation Place makes a distinction between what he calls 'child data' (what is happening within the corporeal body) and 'data child' (the visible manifestation of that corporeality through its connection to the surrounding technological artefacts). The coincidence of the two cannot be taken for granted and it is argued that the conditions whereby they are held together are accomplished minute by minute. He argues that the work of the intensive care unit entails maintaining an association between 'child data' and 'data child'.

Lee (2000) takes a similar approach to a different set of circumstances. He is concerned with the introduction of video testimony by children in abuse cases. He argues that the introduction of this practice in UK courts is not well explained by a general cultural shift in the appreciation of children's capacity as witnesses. Rather there was a dual shift in the mediations between children and courts. On the one hand, medical claims to speak for children's bodies were diminished through the (at least partial) discrediting of the anal dilation reflex test during the Cleveland Enquiry into child abuse accusations. At the same time, technologies were brought into play which helped to overcome long-standing legal objections to children as proper witnesses, objections which he argues are only one instance of a general procedure used to test the credibility of all witnesses. In creating a new alliance between child and device, video arrangements constitute children as proper witnesses and construct them as speaking subjects in this setting.

Place's and Lee's insights give a fresh perspective on Turner's central divide between foundational and non-foundational views; the body and its representations are not mutually exclusive but mutually dependent, embedded in heterogeneous networks. These concerns are well developed within actor–network theory (see, for example, Latour, 1993; Latour and Woolgar, 1986). Sometimes called the sociology of translation, this literature is, as we have seen (see Chapter 3), concerned with the materials from which social life is produced and the practices by which these are ordered and patterned. Being substantively interested in science and technology, its object constantly undermines a sharp distinction between culture and nature by focusing on the network of mediations between them. The sociology of translation has much in common with forms of sociology which emphasize the relational, constructed and processual character of social life. At the same time it is quite distinct in one crucial and radical respect: it rejects the assumption that society is constructed through human action and meaning alone. In this feature it is sharply different from social constructionism. It remains constructivist – but in a radically generalized way; and it restates materialist sociology but in a way which places the material in relation to the other elements that constitute society. In fact 'society' is seen as produced in and through patterned networks of heterogeneous materials; it is made up through a wide variety of shifting associations (and dissociations) between human *and* non-human entities. Indeed, so ubiquitous are associations between humans and the rest of the material world that all entities are to be seen as hybrids – what Latour (1993) has termed 'quasi-objects' and 'quasi-subjects' – where the boundary between the human and the non-human is shifting, negotiated and empirical.

In this view social life cannot, therefore, be reduced either to the 'purely' human (adult or child) or to the 'purely' anything. As a general rule (but subject always to detailed empirical examination) we can say that no entity alone determines the ordering that results from their combination. Sociological approaches which try to make one kind of entity do all the explanatory work result in some form of reductionism – in the way Turner indicates that foundational and non-foundational approaches to the body have a tendency to do. Actor–network theory would see childhoods and bodies, like all phenomena, as constructed not only from human minds and their interactions, not only from human bodies and their interactions, but also through an unending mutually constituting interaction of a vast array of material and non-material resources.

Analysis focuses on the 'translations' – the network of mediations – between these different entities. It is concerned to trace the processes by which these heterogeneous entities mutually enrol, constitute and order each other, processes which always involve something being retained, something being added and something being taken away. Bodies are included – but alongside aspects of the natural and material environment, including their orchestration and hybridization into artefacts of many different types. All of these are to be seen as a priori equal (or symmetrical) actants in the creation of society – or more properly 'the networks of the social'. This approach would place childhoods and bodies in relation to not only symbolic but also material culture. What produces them is not simply biological events, not only the phenomenology of bodily experience, and not merely structures of symbolic meaning – although all of these are important – but also the patterns of material organization and their modes of ordering. Examining childhood bodies in this view becomes a matter of tracing through the materials, practices and processes involved in their construction and maintenance – and in some circumstances their unravelling and disintegration.

Recent attempts to constitute childhood as a sociological topic emphasized it as a social phenomenon in at least two ways: by pointing to the social construction of childhood as a discursive formation and by ethnographic enquiry into the active and creative capacities of children to shape their lives. As with the body, the turn to social constructionism in the sociological study of childhood seemed to wrestle their object away from the assumption that it belongs to the sphere of nature rather than culture. In both cases, however, the attempt to render all things 'social' was problematic. In the sociology of the body it led to theoretical inconsistencies in assumptions about the status of the material body. In addressing these Shilling argued, through his notion of the body unfinished, for an interaction between the body and society and a more open boundary between nature and culture. In the sociology of childhood, the body was at first approached with caution but it became clear that a move similar to Shilling's was necessary. The literature which emerged made sense in terms of the weakening of the culture/nature divide but with some significant modification in the attention to children's own creative activity. In its empirical detail this work revealed the connection between children as social actors and the body and, though emergently, their heterogeneous composition.

Conclusion

Biologists weave narratives about nature. Even though many scientists might wish it were not so, such narratives both draw on and contribute to the cultural resources within their historical time horizon. The complex hybrid of nature and culture through which science is constituted is the condition of all human life, even if we are not able to understand exactly how its different levels merge, interact and relate to each other. Attempts to explain human society only in terms of biology are doomed to reductionist failure but this does not mean that scientists' representations of nature do not also give us glimpses, and sometimes more than that, of how such processes might occur. When biologists begin to accept, as they have, that culture plays an important part in understanding human behaviour then part of the ground for an interdisciplinary dialogue begins to be constructed. Even more importantly when it is recognized that biology and culture might work together and on each other, not as cause and effect, but in a more reciprocal way through complex systems that develop over time, then a step is made towards acknowledging the hybridity of human, including childhood, life. This move takes us away from the additive simplicities of the nature–nurture debate. It begins to recognize and include the 'quasi-subjects' and 'quasi-objects' of which Latour speaks.

Childhood studies, if they are to be a genuinely interdisciplinary field, must step beyond the nature–culture dualism. They cannot claim that childhood is 'cultural' and bracket out all that is 'biological' or vice versa. Retracing the steps of the social means turning back from the cultural reductionism that is involved in making a hard and fast distinction between 'childhood' and 'biological immaturity'. For those working in the social studies of childhood such a reconsideration does not mean abandoning all that has been learnt about childhood from the cultural, social and human historical perspectives. What it does mean is keeping the boundary between nature and culture open. It means, for example, appreciating that extended juvenility forms part of our history as a species and is something that we share with other primates, and perhaps even more distantly with other mammals. In this perspective childhood can be seen not as an epiphenomenon of biology but as translation of it into culture. All childhoods are, in part, constituted through such extended juvenility and all human cultures have to negotiate with it. Because its translation into culture can be accomplished in many different ways, which accrete and leave traces through their history, childhood emerges as a very diverse phenomenon. Within this the body plays an important role, both working on and being worked on by society. The body belongs purely to neither culture nor nature, especially when viewed alongside the technologies that flow through it. In the next chapter I will discuss examples of such bio-social-technical hybrids in relation to childhood.

5 The future of childhood

It is very simple. In the universe, anything can turn into anything else when you have the right formula. So you can be a person one minute and a machine the next minute.

(Nine-year-old American child quoted in Turkle, 1998: 327)

Introduction

In his essay *What Children Say* (1997) the philosopher Gilles Deleuze observes that children frequently maintain a continuous stream of talk about whatever activity they are engaged in. Their activities, he suggests, can be seen as dynamic trajectories of practice and their talk as constructing mental maps of these trajectories. Children's auto-conversations provide an example of how human selves come into being through an unending process of emergence. Children strive to become what they desire to be, creating what Deleuze terms a 'line (or plane) of immanence'. The creation of this line involves a dual activity. Children plot a trajectory that negotiates the more rigid, settled structures and expectations that surround them, what Deleuze calls 'line (or plane) of organization'. This includes such things as the family and the school, which are (relatively) segmented into separate institutions, or territories, each with their own rules and norms of behaviour. In general terms these rules operate by creating mutually exclusive dichotomies: culture and nature; male and female; child and adult; home and school. These strive to shape children, to fix them into 'normal' patterns – thus limiting their desire and creativity but, simultaneously, creating stability and thus making the world appear more certain and less fearful. In the process children are incorporated into the plane of organization (which imposes its expectations of normality upon them) but they also plot 'flights' away from it. This transforms them, allows them to enter into new forms of expression and content and thus create something new as the process goes along. Such lines of immanence tend to dissolve these segmentations and binary divisions, ignoring and hybridizing them and creating new entities.

This discussion of children exemplifies a more general set of concepts that he has developed over numerous writings, often in collaboration with

Felix Guattari (see especially Deleuze and Guattari, 1988). Although it is not possible to summarize the very complex and lengthy arguments that they make, it is notable that Deleuze and Guattari's vision parallels and echoes many theoretical themes discussed in earlier chapters. These include ideas from ANT, Haraway's writings about cyborgs and complexity theory. These concepts are appropriate to the themes and issues discussed in this chapter because they help to focus attention on the emergence of new forms of childhood, or potential childhoods (and their concomitant adult–child relations). In particular the chapter will discuss the disturbance to child–adult relations that novel intersections of 'social', 'biological' and 'technological' networks create – or, to be more precise, the possibilities for childhood in the intermingling of these spheres and their dissolution as distinct territories.

The key idea, which each of the theoretical resources discussed in earlier chapters shares with Deleuze and Guattari, is the heterogeneity of the human world. The world, including its human and social parts, is seen as a set of *assemblages* constituted from heterogeneous elements (Deleuze and Guattari, 1988). The Deleuze–Guattari vision is a very broad one, taking in wide sweeps of human and pre-human history. They offer novel philosophical concepts that draw on and borrow from both the contemporary natural sciences and the arts. A key feature of their writing is a rigorous anti-humanism, their refusal to treat the world as if it were centred on human affairs; that is their debt to Nietzsche. It expresses a post-Darwinian view of human life in which human existence is seen in the context of the evolution of life. The Enlightenment belief in the uniqueness and separateness of humans is no longer regarded as tenable and human life has to be seen in terms of its emergence from, connections with and dependence on the heterogeneous materials that make up the world. Therefore, rather than simply accepting human meaning as the foundation of their analysis they make it problematic. They do this by decentring the human world and seeing it in the context of broader physical and biological processes. Humans are not seen as the sole authors of themselves but as caught up with a multitude of other entities and forces. Deleuze and Guattari distinguish three main types entity: the physico-chemical (which they exemplify through a discussion of crystals), the organic (which they exemplify by DNA sequences) and the anthropomorphic (or human-like). Each of these is seen as contributing to the emergence and construction of human social life. However, these different strata of reality follow somewhat different logics of action and becoming. So, for example, the macroscopic form of crystals is mechanically *induced* from their molecular properties. The protein sequences through which different forms of animal and plant life emerge are created by being *transduced* (or brought across) by their matching DNA. However, the anthropomorphic stratum is marked by the more complex and transformative process of *translation*, through which elements of the physico-chemical and organic strata are incorporated into the anthropomorphic one and vice-versa. Once again their approach can thus be seen to overlap with the themes discussed in earlier chapters of this book.

Deleuze and Guattari's discussion pays a great deal of attention to characteristics of the human species such as technology and language. In line with the anthropological thinking discussed in Chapter 4, they see the emergence of the human species as involving the modification of the function of the hand and the mouth in a way that makes possible the use of tools and language. This led to the creation of both what Deleuze and Guattari term a 'social technological machine' (an ensemble of 'man–tool–animal–thing') and a 'semiotic machine' (or 'regime of signs'). These assemble heterogeneous materials – humans, animals, plants, minerals – in networks that mediate nature and culture and which produce new capacities to act and hence new fields of power. What it is to be human is thus decentred. Rather than seeing humans as isolated from the world, human capacities and powers derive from their connection with it. Human history is the process of borrowing from the non-human world, creating new combinations and new extensions of the body (and, as we shall see, the mind).

Their most striking historical examples of this are found in a discussion of the various alliances between humans and horse that created new assemblages and new powers. The combination of human, horse and stirrup, for example, extended the distances that people could travel. The human–horse–sword assemblage extended the fighting capacity of the arm and thus created new military powers. The human–horse–plough extended the human capacity to till land and thus created new powers to farm, the potential to trade and, eventually, to create settlements. In this process both the human and the horse became changed. Deleuze and Guattari use the metaphor of the 'rhizome' to express the idea of the world as a complex set of assemblages that constantly proliferate, iterate, bifurcate, combine, transform and perform (in a manner similar to that discussed by complexity theory). Rhizome is a botanical term for a low-lying or underground stem (the strawberry plant is a familiar example) that, by putting out tendrils, forms a complex, multi-branched, bifurcating but interconnecting structure. As an image of social life it counters mechanical notions of hierarchical and stable structure by drawing attention to its dynamic properties. But, unlike the strawberry plant which transforms the physico-chemical into only one kind of organic product, rhizomes in the anthropomorphic strata potentiate multitudes of lines of organization and lines of immanence, proliferating all sorts of new entities, beings, techniques, problems and paradoxes (see also De Landa, 1997).

In recommending Deleuze and Guattari as a framework for thinking about childhood I am following Lee (2001a: 115) who suggests:

> humans find themselves in an open-ended swirl of extensions and supplementations, changing their powers and characteristics as they

pass through different assemblages . . . Looking through Deleuze and Guattari's . . . eyes we do not see a single incomplete natural order waiting to be finished by human beings, we see many incomplete orderings that remain open to change . . . a picture of human life, whether adult or child, as an involvement in multiple becomings . . . Deleuze and Guattari have given us a framework within which to compare . . . various childhoods . . . Whether children are in or out of place, or whether new places are being made for them, we can ask what assemblages they are involved in and what extensions they are living through.

He shows how this might work by discussing various examples. Brazilian street children, for instance, are understood as an assemblage of 'child–group–street' that comes into conflict with another assemblage of 'police–law–state'. Current efforts to introduce curfews on children in the UK are seen as the state promoting the 'parents–child–house' assemblage over the 'child–group–street' assemblage. In fact various of the trends discussed in Chapter 1 can be put into fresh perspective when they are viewed as assemblages. The ways in which the contemporary media are pluralizing socialization can be seen as a clash between a 'classroom–teacher–child' assemblage and a 'child–television–marketplace' one and the UN Convention on the Rights of the Child can be understood as an attempt to put together a new assemblage around children that protects children without claiming complete ownership of them.

Children and mundane artefacts

These are all instructive examples and I intend in this chapter to pursue the analysis of childhoods as assemblages begun by Lee by taking it into some further areas. I will discuss information and communication technology, reproductive and genetic technologies, and neuropharmocological substances, chosen because each speaks to potential emergent assemblages with broad implications for the future of childhood. However, before moving on to this I want to amplify the discussion so far by pointing the discussion away from exotic and new technologies and towards the way artefacts form a very important part of the everyday worlds of children. Such everyday worlds have been at the centre of recent social studies of childhood, where they have been explored to discover the mundane and often overlooked ways in which children participate in social life and exercise agency. However, these investigations have seldom looked at everyday life in terms of their heterogeneous assembly or the manner in which children form alliances with other entities and through which their agentic powers are created.

The population of children's everyday lives by artefacts emerged strongly in a recent exploratory study of 'techno-toys' (Plowman *et al.*, 2003; see also Plowman and Luckin, 2003). This term was used to refer to toys, such as robot dogs or interactive dolls, which use digital technology to make them responsive to and interactive with the children who use them. Such toys now regularly feature among the annual lists of best-sellers and have become the focus of much moral concern. Critics argue that by encoding only a limited range of responses they threaten to erode children's creative play (Levin and Rosenquest, 2001). However, the study showed that, perhaps unlike the older generation for whom they have novelty, contemporary children do not regard these toys as fundamentally different from more traditional toys and generally use them in similar ways:

> Another interesting process through which normalisation of techno-toys takes place is through the children's use of the techno-toy on their own terms . . . Children may play with it in their own imagined ways by ignoring completely the features which prescribe the type of inter-action or using them in innovative ways.
>
> (Plowman *et al.*, 2003)

In fact, for the children one of the most important features of a toy was not so much its digital interactivity as its capacity to give them access to a network of other children. Rather than abandon their playmates to isolate themselves with the toy, children take the techno-toy to the playground or try and reach the outside group of players. The toy is thus used as a way of being enrolled or enrolling others.

This possibility is highlighted and extended in Ogilvie-Whyte's (2003) current ethnography of Scottish children's interactions with each other in various play activities. Guided by insights drawn from ANT (see Chapters 3 and 4) her observational work in a children's playground reveals children as 'heterogeneous engineers'. In their interactions with each other, and in pursuit of their interests as they emerge through these interactional processes, they enrol and orchestrate all kinds of human and non-human entities. In an extended example of a conflict between two groups over who will have use of the playground she shows how the opposing groups of children tactically and strategically deploy a large range of human and non-human entities. These include older children, siblings and parents but also balls, planks of wood and a dog! She comments:

> In the micro setting of the Hillend playground it becomes more than apparent that the majority of social relations are held together in the interaction of humans and non-humans. A cursory glance shows that the landscape of the playground is characterized by small groups of children – each group bound together by an object or objects of sorts. The types of objects are diverse indeed – footballs, beyblades, beyblade stadiums, skateboards, inline skates, wrestling figures and wrestling rings, Barbie dolls, Gameboys and so on.
>
> (Ogilvie-Whyte, 2003)

These artefacts, she shows, are not merely props for social interaction but are embedded in and part of the social just as much as are other humans. However, throughout her ethnography she explores how the field of possibilities from which children can draw such supplements and extensions is limited. Some people and things are not available to some children but are available to others and it is often, she argues, these limitations that shape the outcome of interactions, especially the struggles that children engage in with each other and with adults. One example of this is the persistent attempt of boys to smuggle trainers into school. These were crucial to boys' ability to take part in the informal but competitive football games that were central to their relationships with each other. So important were these to their ability to perform skilfully that they were willing to risk the wrath of parents and the punishments of school (where trainers were banned). She comments:

> in their discussions of such issues (whether it be football boots, trainers or any other things) children have an implicit recognition that they can extend their agency as collective in some senses. At times they recognize that they can extend their agency through assemblages with some actants but also that, likewise, some assemblages – some actants – may impair their agentic powers.
>
> (Ogilvie-Whyte, 2003)

This illustrates the Deleuze and Guattari point that assemblages supplement and extend human capacities in ways that open up new powers and possibilities, including variations in the way both inter- and intra-generational relations are constructed (see Chapter 3). As we will see in the examples discussed below, such processes also open up new debates, controversies and problems.

Information and communication technologies

In Chapter 1 we saw that since the 1970s there has been concern about how technologies such as television are changing the character of childhood. In fact, of course, concerns about the supposed effect of new technologies on children have a provenance that stretches back at least to the start of the twentieth century, since when radio, cinema, comics, music records, computer games and videos have all been accused of corrupting the young. As today, these accusations are likely to come from both the left and the right of the political spectrum, although political conservatives are more likely to frame these in terms of moral decline and those from the left more likely to see them as capitalist conspiracies (Barker, 1984; Kline, 1995). However, in order to see how such debates arise from novel assemblages rather than from the unique properties of 'new technology', it is worth reminding ourselves of examples such as that given by Murdock and McCron (1979). They quote the following denunciation of popular theatre made in the *Edinburgh Review* in 1851:

> One powerful agent for the depraving of the boyish classes of our towns and cities is to be found in the cheap shows and theatres, which are so specially chosen and arranged for the attraction of the young . . . it is not to be wondered at that the boy who is led to haunt them becomes so rapidly corrupted and demoralized, and seeks to be the doer of the infamies which have interested him as a spectator.

Such discourses are commonplace and persist (though in new forms) today, for example, around the supposed ill effects of the internet. However, as suggested in Chapter 1, in the 1970s a different and more fundamental sort of claim began to appear. Critics, such as Postman (1983) and Winn (1984), have argued that new media, especially television, are not merely corrupting the young but are breaking down the distinction between children and adults such that the whole institution of childhood is 'disappearing'. TV and other communication technologies do this, it is claimed, by opening up 'adult' information and values and making them available to children, a trend that alarms some observers. More recently a counter discourse (for example, Katz, 1997) has developed, in which contemporary digital technologies, such as the PC and the internet, are assigned a positive value in their relationship to child–adult relationships. Children are hailed as the bearers, indeed the avant garde, of a new set of historical possibilities in economy and society. Included in this is a breakdown of the binary distinction between childhood and adulthood that is welcomed and embraced.

The difference between these two positions is often summarized by the use of terms such as 'cyber-critics' and 'cyber-utopians' and both positions have been criticized for essentializing the category child, underestimating differences between children, denying children's capacity to be social actors and for employing technologically determinist arguments (Buckingham, 2000; Holloway and Valentine, 2001). However, Selwyn (2003) has recently shown that the discourses around children and information and communication technology (ICT) are considerably more complex than this two-fold division indicates. He has examined how broadcast media, commercial advertising of ICT and UK policy documents have represented the issues and suggests that six different discourses can be identified. These are:

- children as 'naturally adept users of technology';
- information transforming ordinary children into exceptionally skilled ones (by somehow boosting, for example, their reading and maths skills);
- computers transforming children so that they become adept at 'adult' activities (such as running businesses or dealing in stocks and shares);

- deviant children who seek out 'adult' material on the internet or through computer games;
- innocent children who are exposed to inappropriate violent or sexual material through their use of information technology;
- children's need to use IT because it will fit them for the information society and network economy.

This analysis shows that contemporary debates about ICT cannot be made to fit with an oppositional dichotomy between critics and utopians. There is considerable ambiguity in public discussion that cannot be easily reduced to just two positions. However, these extreme positions have become politicized such that the more complex ground between them is obscured. Although their views are passionately held, neither side of the argument can ground their views in research adequate to the certainty of their own beliefs (Buckingham, 2000) and in any case such strongly held views are resistant to the evidence, such as it is. In fact, research in children's use of ICT is fraught with methodological difficulties that will not yield simple answers to simplistic questions such as what the 'effects' of ICT use are. However, the tendency of research that has actually examined how children use, understand, are affected by and act towards ICT is to undermine both extreme positions (see, for example, Bingham *et al.*, 1999; Facer *et al.*, 2001a) by grounding them in the practical realities of children's ICT use.

So, for instance, Valentine and Holloway (2002) have investigated how children use ICT and what part it plays in the construction of their identities. Using questionnaires, diaries, focus groups, semi-structured interviews and online interviews, they show how children reconstruct and reconfigure their social relationships and identities in online spaces. Their main conclusion is that 'their "virtual" activities are not in practice, disconnected from their off-line identities and relationships . . . on-line and off-line identities are not oppositional or unconnected but are mutually constituted' (Valentine and Holloway, 2002: 316). They identify a number of processes through which ICT activities and the children's everyday lives are mutually constitutive. For example, online identities are contingent upon and/or reproduce already present class and gender inequalities. Information gleaned through online activities is incorporated into their offline ones (for instance, by feeding into their hobbies and interests). It is also clear from this work that different children use the internet in different ways:

[F]or some children it emerges as a tool to develop intimate on-line friendships, while for others it emerges as a tool of sociality that develops everyday off-line social networks: for some it emerges as an important tool for developing off-line hobbies, and for others as a casual tool for larking about.

(Valentine and Holloway, 2002: 316)

This underlines another key point inherent in the ideas of Deleuze and Guattari (and ANT). Just as what it means to be a child cannot be essentialized into some unchanging, stable entity, so what an ICT 'is' shifts according to the assemblage within which it performs. Its context and its connections with other human and non-human endlessly constructs and reconstructs it, such that the 'child–computer' assemblage is an emergent entity not stabilized in its properties or effects.

What then is the meaning of ICT and related artefacts for childhood? Selwyn (2003) suggests that much of the current debate makes a mistake in seeing the issue primarily in terms of child–adult relationships. He suggests that underlying the public discussion are economic and political interests. ICT companies, for example, may use images of children but their primary motive lies in selling information technology hardware and software to the adults who have the resources to buy them (even though it may be children who use them most). Governments, he points out, are interested in persuading populations that they must bow to the demands of a competitive, information-based economy. However, although these multiple interests in selling IT are important, their recognition is not inconsistent with the idea that ICT creates new possibilities for generational relationships. Indeed the wide-ranging debates that Selwyn documents, as well as the fervour of both the cyber-critics and the cyber-utopians, seem to betoken that something important is happening in the reconfiguration of adult–child relationships and that technology is implicated in it, even if it does not directly or solely cause it.

The observation that information and communication technologies are implicated in the forging of new social and economic relations has, of course, been widely made by social theorists. Pre-eminent among these is the name of Manuel Castells. In volume 1 of his *Rise of Network Society*, Castells (2000) analyses the new economic forms that he sees as emerging from information technology. The 'network economy', he argues, uses information as its primary raw material, acting on it through technologies that deploy and produce a networking logic. Information generation, processing and transmission are the basic resources of emergent, contemporary forms of power that, according to Castells, are coming to dominate the world economy. This new power does not reside in capitalist firms or the state but in diffused codes of information, and the representations and identities that are constructed through it. In this process new forms of identity politics are generated, often through resistance and opposition. All kinds of movements resist the logic of network society: religious fundamentalism, nationalism, ethnicity, localism, environmentalism, feminism and sexual identity movements. It is these conflicts, he argues, that are displacing traditional political parties, as well as struggles between labour and capital, creating new social movements and forcing a crisis in the nation state and its established forms of democracy. At the same time a new dimension of conflict is being forged between the new elites, who can access the high-speed mobility that electronic networks afford, and those who are bound by traditional constraints of physical time and space. This presents a rather pessimistic prospectus for the social movements articulating the interests of movements and minority groups. Such groups stand in danger of being excluded because they are not folded into the electronic networks that are the new sources of power in the world.

A somewhat different approach is taken by the Italian philosopher Gianni Vattimo (1992). He suggests that new and emerging information and communication technologies will have the effect of creating a voice for individuals and social groups who previously did not have one. He proposes that the mass media have played a decisive role in bringing the modern period to an end by ushering in an era of 'generalized communication'. Vattimo connects the proliferation of communication with the emergence of pluralism. Everything becomes an object of communication because the mass media generate an enormous, never-ending demand for 'stories' that they can retail. This fragments and breaks up any attempt to unify narratives and histories. Potentially everyone and every group have a story to tell and a different way of recounting their historical experience. Vattimo pays particular attention to the perspectives of those living in the formerly colonized parts of the world, whose struggles to liberate themselves from imperial rule more or less coincided with the growth of the mass media and a global communications technology. However, we can also see how many previously marginalized groups, whose perspectives were excluded from the modernist account of ever greater rationalization and progress, have been articulated during the second half of the twentieth century. They include, for example, the black people's anti-racist movement, the women's movement and gay people. However, as Vattimo is quick to point out, the proliferation and pluralization of communication does not lead to a 'transparent' society. Rather it produces a much greater complexity of points of view, a veritable Tower of Babel that tends towards the chaotic. The internet appears in many ways to be a model of Vattimo's analysis of the society of generalized communication. The much-vaunted 'anarchy' of the internet means that many different voices can speak. Every group, whatever its ideology, can stake out a place and its message can be made available for those who want to search it out, as for those who just happen to stumble across it.

Lee (2001b) addresses these issues from the point of view of childhood. He notes that the late-twentieth century has seen the emergence of the idea that children are people who have their own perspectives and that, concomitant with this, childhood studies have taken on board the social constitution of childhood and the status of children as social actors (see also Chapters 2 and 3). He then asks why these ideas arose at the time that they did. His answer concerns the emergence of the possibility of thinking about children in terms other than as appendages to the families, schools and welfare institutions. Their dependencies on adults were rethought through, to use Thorne's phrase, 'the conceptual autonomy of childhood' (1987). Throughout modernity, he argues, it did make good sense to understand children through notions of dependency. This way of thinking reflected the manner in which childhood was constructed as a 'cocooned' state, as children were wrapped up in layers of protection, including the family, the home, the school and welfare institutions. However, towards the end of the twentieth century this set of arrangements began to unravel (see Chapter 1). The strong boundary around the family home, constituting it as a private sphere, began to weaken. The growing entry of women into the labour market significantly affected the division between the public, secular world of work, which had previously been monopolized by men, and the private, 'sacred' sphere of the family. As Lee (2001b) notes:

> The form of patriarchy practised in the family home was dependent on the sustainability of men's position as exclusive interface between the family and the world of production. As long as productive work belonged to men, and as long as men could rely on finding employment, the family home could remain a place of 'innocence' and all within it could remain trivial. The private, secret space of the family home involved an infantalisation of children as much as it did an infantalisation of women.

While the public and private spheres had always been connected, the mechanisms by which this was rendered were relatively invisible. The home, however, was changing not only in terms of production but it also became the locus for the consumption of new sorts of technologies. Some of these, especially the 'labour saving' ones such as the refrigerator and the washing machine, responded to but also helped to make possible the emergence of a new division of labour between men and women. This created the possibility of further and broader forms of consumption and with this arose ideas of choice and decision-making. TV and other ICTs played a role in this, conveying into the 'private' sphere of the home ideas about consumer choice, as well as information and values about a multitude of other topics. So it was that one of the oppositional dichotomies, through which modern childhood was represented and constructed, began to weaken.

Children (and organizations advocating children's perspectives) have certainly taken up some of the possibilities that this offers. For example, if one enters the term 'children's rights' in to the Google search engine of a PC, it produces over four-and-a-half million hits. The spectrum of organizations and interests represented is worldwide and it is remarkable how many groups and organizations seeking to promote the idea of children's rights have chosen the internet as a vehicle for doing so.

However, there are good reasons to believe that the line between new technology and the emergence of a children's identity politics is not as straightforward as it might appear. First, the internet reveals not a unitary politics of childhood but a variety of different views about many different issues. While most sites promote the idea of children's participation in social life, the internet emerges primarily as a conduit for many varied social and political stances. Some, for example, advocate children's rights as a way of wrapping up other, rather different interests. For example, it is used as a rhetoric for advancing fathers' rights during divorce proceedings and promoting anti-abortion causes. Even among those that advocate children's rights in a more direct fashion there are many different perspectives, reflecting all kinds of differences between children. There is here no single 'voice of the child' but a multiplicity of overlapping and conflicting ones. Second, the vast number of sites reflects the chaotic tendency of generalized communication that Vattimo writes about. This, indeed, appears as a Tower of Babel in which many speak but few listen, and even fewer understand. Third, while the internet may encourage the voicing of many points of view, it is not at all clear that this is reflected in other forms of mass media. TV, radio and newspapers remain highly important parts of the public space within which social and political issues are debated (see, for example, Davis and Bourhill, 1997, on the demonization of children in the UK press; see also Higonnet, 1998; Holland, 1992). Fourth, children's access to ICTs is not uncontested. Facer *et al.* (2001b) show how mundane domestic arrangements, like where the PC is placed within the home, influence how children are able to use it. Parental fears about what children might encounter on the internet temper children's internet use by making it subject to their surveillance. The software industry has not been slow in providing the means by which machines can be set up to filter out content that might be thought harmful. Finally, as Castells is at pains to argue, electronic networks create new patterns of exclusion and inequality. Some individuals, groups and societies have much more access than others and networks both connect and disconnect. Castells (2000, vol. 3) argues that the collapse of the Soviet Union was caused largely because it was not able to enter information networks in a way that, say, the Pacific region clearly was. Large parts of the Third World in Africa, Asia and South America and the poorest parts of the developed world (see also Facer *et al.*, 2001b) form a kind of underclass in informational terms. To a large degree information technology is more likely to convey children in these regions into drugs and prostitution than it is to give them a voice in a new political discourse.

So the outcome of the encounter between childhood and ICTs is uncertain and still emergent. It is clear, however, that whatever direction it takes in the future, it has, for the moment, begun to create shifts in children's position and the character of childhood. Children who are connected with TV and the internet extend the reach of their experience and multiply the range of the facts and values they encounter. As we have seen, this occurs within the context of their existing everyday lives and not as a disjuncture from it, suggesting that it can be played out in many different ways. Some of these will reproduce existing relationships and others will create new directions and possibilities. Because it has a rhizomic character, this process is best understood as being driven by multiple influences. In this respect those who argue that a single technology, whether it be TV (as in Postman) or the internet (as in Katz), is bringing about a change in the conditions of childhood are wrong. Devices and technologies are not inserted into social relations from the outside. They are created and create effects within a particular social and economic context and it is to this whole network of connections that we must look if we are to grasp the process. This suggests that the 'effects' of new information and communications technologies will not fold into childhood in any simple or uncontested way.

It is clear from the discussion so far that new socio-technical assemblages can extend children's reach into worlds of ideas and information previously unavailable to them, giving them the potential power to multiply these beyond those contained within the physical and temporal boundaries of their everyday locales. Perhaps, however, it is necessary to take a much broader view of the way the ICTs discussed above are entering into the construction of childhood. Haraway (1991) opens just such a possibility in her argument for the idea of the 'cyborg', a term that conjoins 'cyber' and 'organism' to indicate an entity that is part human and part technological. Haraway suggests that cyborgs are a relatively new, postmodern phenomenon, although the perspective taken in this book would suggest that the connection between humans and machines is a long-standing historical (and pre-historical) phenomenon. Nevertheless, it provides both children and adults with resources for thinking about familiar human experiences in new terms. For example, Turkle's (1997, 1998) longitudinal ethnographic work on children's interactions with computers shows how they have over time raised different questions about and developed different understandings of whether machines have consciousness. When children first encountered computer-based games and toys, and in the US this was generally during the 1980s, their properties were puzzling for children. She comments that:

> Confronted with objects that spoke, strategised and 'won', children were led to argue the moral and metaphysical status of machines on the basis of their psychologies. Did the machines know what they were doing? Did they have intentions, consciousness and feelings? These first computers that entered children's lives were evocative objects: they became the occasion for new formulations about the human and the mechanical . . . a first generation of children who were willing to invest machines with qualities of consciousness as they rethought the question of what is alive in the context of 'machines that think'.
>
> (Turkle, 1998: 318)

This, she argues, disrupted the conventional Piagetian account of how children come to distinguish living from non-living things. Piaget, of course, inhabited a world in which such a distinction was a given. From an anthropological point of view, however, 'things' with life might be thought a rather common phenomenon in the record of human cultures, although not in modernity, which as we have seen throughout this book, required a more exclusive separation. Nevertheless, for the children of the 1980s the question of machines with consciousness became a topic of dispute, animating conversation among playmates. Some believed they were 'just machines' and could not have psychological characteristics, while others disagreed. By the end of the 1990s, however, such disputes had, according to Turkle's fieldwork, all but disappeared from children's conversations. Instead there was an acceptance of a much more fuzzy and fluid boundary between the living and the non-living, the conscious and the non-conscious. Computers are 'sort of alive' or made of 'computer cy-dough-plasm'. Far from being immature in their thinking, which a Piagetian framework might be taken to imply, these children have led the way in accepting the hybrid, heterogeneous character of things, able to 'cycle' through a range of possibilities and ambivalences at high speed. As one nine-year-old child explained: 'It is very simple. In the universe, anything can turn into anything else when you have the right formula. So you can be a person one minute and a machine the next minute.'

Reproductive technology

It is, however, not only children's own discourse that has become infused with cyborg metaphors. Croissant (1998: 285–300) shows how contemporary accounts of the development of children's motor learning and development are expressed through an 'open loop' and 'closed loop' language derived from cybernetics and linked to sports science models of perfecting the body as a performing, properly maintained machine. At the same time the Humanoid Robotics Group at MIT is building a robot (named Cog) that will contain a 'baby brain', which will mimic the human child by being born with certain basic behaviours, including bonding with a 'mother' and the ability to respond to cross-culturally present human bodily cues such as smiling and frowning. Current developments, the robot builders tell us, include the following:

> To date neither Cog nor Lazlo have faces. Our goal is to design and fabricate an iconic, humanoid face for each robot that fosters a suitable social contract between the robot and humans. Another goal of this project is to shift the robot aesthetic to a design language that utilizes strong curvilinear and organic forms through state of the art design processes and materials. With a well designed face, Cog and Lazlo will be able to convey an appropriate social aspect. This will assist them in

regulating interaction, receiving appropriate stimulus and, in the longer term, learning imitation tasks.

(Humanoid Robotics Group, 2003)

While these examples seem to belong to science fiction, it is only an appearance. Whatever the outcome, these are real, well-financed and high status technological developments. So whatever the future holds, they alert us to the fact that the processes through which many children come into the world are *already* marked by a multitude of hybrid human–technical processes. For example, in the UK and the US the following procedures are frequently part of a routine pregnancy and birth: a battery of tests and screening procedures for various medical and genetic conditions, and fetal abnormalities, including the use of chorionic villus sampling and amniocentesis: ultrasound scanning; fetal heart rate monitoring; checks on the volume of amniotic fluid; the use of forceps or a vacuum extractor, pain relieving drugs, administered intravenously, locally or by use of an epidural or spinal block; the acceleration of delivery through oxytocin, pitocin, prostaglandin or misoprostol and a surgical episiotomy or caesarian section. On birth the umbilical cord will be cut with sterile instruments and various antibiotic substances applied to the baby. Among the diseases that are routinely tested for at birth are phenylketonuria, galactosemia, sickle-cell anemia and thyroid deficiency. In the first year of life a battery of developmental milestones will be monitored and a variety of immunizations given (including those against hepatitus B, diphtheria, tetanus and pertussis, influenza, measles, mumps, rubella and varicella) and so on. Before, during and after our birth, our being and our becoming entails not only the collectivities that signify social relations but also a vast entanglement of socio-technical networks.

Over the last 30 years historians and sociologists, especially feminist ones, have explored, documented and analysed reproductive technologies (see Coward, 1989; Ehrenreich and English, 1993; Martin, 1990; Oakley, 1984; and Wajcman, 1991). This, for reasons to do with the growth of the feminist movement, is largely concerned with women and their experience of pregnancy and birth. In part, however, this discussion grappled with questions about how to understand the role of technology in social life. The trajectory of this work reflects an increasingly complex understanding of the relationship between technology and society. At first, technology is essentialized, seen as fixed and given though open to abuse by the powerful, especially men. At a later stage technology is seen as socially shaped – as created in the social world and moulded by competing interests. Finally, society and technology become seen as co-constitutive, and technology is starting to be seen as a hybrid of nature and culture. Interests are inscribed in it but these are ambiguous and shifting rather than fixed and given (see, for example, Davis-Floyd and Dumit, 1998).

These conceptual issues were also played in relation to other emerging reproductive technologies, especially those of assisted conception (such as *in vitro* fertilization, surrogacy and egg donation) and pre-natal testing and screening (such as ultra-sound and amniocentesis, see p. 127). Although, in the 1970s Firestone (1972: 193) suggested from a radical feminist position that technology could liberate women from the 'tyranny of reproduction', a main line of argument has been to see assisted reproduction as a continuation of patriarchal attempts to control pregnancy and childbirth. Women's bodies, it has been argued, are being expropriated, objectified, fragmented, and subjected to risky, ineffective and degrading treatments (Corea *et al.*, 1985). The driving force and end result of this process is seen as male control of human creation that will render women unnecessary. However, although the dangers of reproductive technology are recognized, for many feminists this is an overdrawn picture. Stanworth (1987), for example, suggests that the technologies of assisted reproduction are, not withstanding their enmeshment in systems of medical domination, beneficial for some women. Women, it is suggested, are not passive in relation to their use and, rather than oppose them on principle, should articulate their own interests and purposes in relation to them.

This difference of opinion highlights the inadequacy of its own essentialized terms. Rather than seeing 'technology', 'women' and 'men' as fixed, unambiguous entities it is more helpful to see them as mutually implicated and emergent. Reproductive technologies are not neutral, they are shaped by and express social and political interests − but it is not necessary to see this in terms of monolithic conspiracies (of men or anyone else). They involve different assemblages of materials, and social and discursive practices, which take place across different contexts. The complexity and open-endedness of these processes mean that the 'same' technology can generate many different, contradictory, paradoxical, unintended and unexpected meanings and effects. As Treichler (1990) has argued this multiplies and destabilizes the categories of events and persons in the world. For example, she points out how reproductive technologies have complicated the term 'mother'. Discourse, both popular and medical, now abounds with hybrid mothers: 'egg mother', 'birth mother', 'name mother', 'surrogate mother', 'gene mother', 'biomother', 'adoptive mother', 'foster mother', 'legal mother', 'organ mother', 'nurturant mother' and 'earth mother' are some of the examples she has found.

Genetic testing, choice and children

However, it will be noticed that most of the discussion of reproductive technology that has occurred over the last 20 or 30 years concentrates on its implications for women and, more broadly, for gender relations. Children, childhood and generational relations more generally appear as an adjunct to that gender-based discussion. However, woven through the exploration of reproductive technologies there is a series of issues that directly and indirectly implicate children and childhood. Some of these concern now routine technologies (such as antenatal testing and screening), while others are linked to emergent technologies (such as genetic medicine and human cloning).

Although these do raise new issues, it is important to note that their discussion often finds parallels in existing human experience. First, there are already a number of issues that arise around children's relationship to genetic testing. Conditions such as Huntingdon's disease are genetically transmitted (through a single dominant gene) but do not have serious consequences for health until later life. Pre-symptomatic testing raises a host of problems when the person being tested is a child. These hinge around whether or not it is judged better to know that one has the disease in advance of its effects being felt, especially in cases where treatment does not exist or is uncertainly effective. Disclosure involves risks such as provoking depression and anxiety. For this reason such testing is generally subject to the informed consent of the individual concerned. Informed consent, however, depends on the individual being deemed competent to understand the consequences of taking the test. The social and legal position of children complicates this issue and makes it subject to contestation. Alderson (1993) argues that children who have lived with chronic illness, or the awareness of its possibility, develop high levels of awareness and understanding. In common with demonstrations of children's competence in general, this is often remarked upon as 'surprising', a reaction that indicates the strength and ubiquity of stereotyped attitudes to children. This is underlined by Dickenson's (1999) argument that although UK law permits children who have been able to demonstrate competence to give their consent to testing, it is a widespread practice among testing agencies to refuse it to those under the age of majority (which is 18 in the UK).

Second, childhood is implicated in the kinds of antenatal testing and screening mentioned above. They are intended to give potential parents information about whether or not a pregnancy will result in a disabled child. Women who do not attend antenatal clinics or who refuse the tests available are likely to be seen as problematic and there is strong normative pressure to undergo testing (Press and Browner, 1997). Although the information is often quite limited, being based on probabilities rather than certainties, producing false positives and negatives, and is unable to specify the degree of disability, it nevertheless contributes to discretion about whether to continue with pregnancy or whether to abort the foetus. According to Rothman (1988) this reconstitutes pregnancy as 'tentative' until the tests have given the 'all clear'. The issues raised by existing technologies of antenatal testing are likely to be intensified if emerging techniques of pre-implantation genetic testing become available. In these, cells are removed from embryos created *in vitro* and tested for genetic disorders before being implanted in the uterus. This is already used to test for cystic fibrosis and Down syndrome. In the UK it is strongly regulated but in the US and some European countries it is used to select the sex of a future baby. It is likely to become more common in future and the range of conditions and characteristics that can be tested for will expand.

Clearly such antenatal testing and screening has eugenic implications. These are rather different from those that occurred earlier in the twentieth century but they still raise issues about the kinds and range of people who will be born into future generations of children. The most notorious eugenic strategies of the past rested on the organized coercion of states, as for example in the Nazi state's mass murder of disabled people or its attempts to selectively breed a 'master race'. In contemporary society, however, eugenic effects emerge as a consequence of individual choice. Each woman or couple might make an individual decision to terminate a pregnancy because the resultant child may be disabled but the overall effect of this will be to select against certain kinds of people – resulting in the 'weak eugenics' that Shakespeare (1998) argues is what is emerging from current practice. Medical advocates of antenatal testing (or 'prenatal diagnosis' as it is rather more revealingly termed in the US) promote it in terms of an 'optimistic narrative' of choice and the conquest of disease but underlying this is a 'pessimistic narrative' that assumes the lives of disabled people are not worth living (Shakespeare, 1999). As Shakespeare points out this depends upon seeing disability as a form of individual impairment and ignoring the extent to which disabled people's lives are made difficult by social discrimination and prejudice.

'Choice' is always embedded in a social context that shapes how it is made and what its consequences will be. Whose choice is being enabled is, therefore, a crucial question. The problems created by antenatal testing are, according to Shakespeare, the result of a multi-sided contest between different 'rights'. Included in these are a woman's right to choose; the civil rights of people with disabilities; the postulated rights of the unborn child; and the rights of society versus the rights of the individual. However, while this captures much of importance in the play between different perspectives, it is also important to recognize that the articulation of rights is a way of constructing and representing interests. Contests of interest, though often wrapped in moral claims, depend for their ongoing outcomes mainly on the play of forces, which are differentially generated, mobilized and deployed by different social groups. The medical profession, for example, is often able to generate a great deal of power through its relatively stable and connected networks. This means it rarely needs to deploy a rhetoric of 'rights', a strategy more associated with the less powerful. Indeed, rights claims can be seen as a way of generating social power when a group has few other resources available to it. Typically such a strategy involves trying to create a unified (and therefore essentialized) identity, a single point of view from which rights are articulated and claimed. This can be effective and has been a strategy employed by many social movements in the twentieth century: women, disabled people, gay and lesbian people are among the examples, although as this list suggests, not with equal success. Inevitably, however, rights strategies also tend to bundle together interests that are not necessarily identical, thus suppressing differences that eventually resurface to destabilize the achievement of a unified identity.

However, while many minority groups can articulate a voice of their own through collective action and hold it together in a more or less unified form long enough to create a political presence, this is difficult in the case of the as-yet-not-born. Their voice can only exist through the translation of others – and this opens the way for this discursive space to be colonized by others. The voice of the unborn therefore emerges in a multitude of contradictory and paradoxical registers. One version constructs it in the language of the religious right, in which the absolute value of life is promoted against all other values and interests (though this tends to be associated only with individual rights, and talk about collective ones, around poverty and exploitation, is muted). Given the religious right's record of repressive social attitudes, this approach has been politically problematic for many advocates of minority rights. The women's movement has argued for abortion under the banner of 'a woman's right to choose' and, notwithstanding arguments about every child being a wanted child, has prioritized women's over fetal rights. However, when antenatal procedures are used to test the sex of the foetus, with the possibility that in many circumstances female foetuses may be aborted, this becomes problematic. For example, is opposition to fetal sex selection to be opposed on the grounds of women's, fetal or children's rights? Shakespeare's opposition to the eugenic drift of antenatal testing draws on both disability and children's rights and it is probably in an elaboration of this that novel developments will take place.

However, the issue of sex selection illustrates another important feature of the current situation. Determining the sex of a foetus has moved from being an uncertain and expensive procedure to a routine and inexpensive one. In fact the availability of cheap ultrasound machines and easy access to abortion has had a marked effect on sex ratios in Asia. In Korea the ratio of boys to girls born is 122:100; in China it is 117:100 (Fukuyama, 2003: 80). This is happening because strong cultural and social pressures are pushing towards the selection of male over female children – just the sort of effect of 'weak', individual choice-driven eugenics that Shakespeare warns against. This individual but culturally shaped set of choices occurs despite the fact that in Korea and China it is illegal to carry out abortions for reasons of sexual selection. There is, then, good reason to believe that when social and cultural choices find a technological means for their fulfilment then governmental regulatory frameworks may be relatively powerless to prevent them.

Engineering the child

That the interplay of technology, society and individual desire (although these are never really separable) produces unintended consequences and can escape regulatory frameworks is a central consideration when thinking about the consequences of humankind's increasing knowledge of the human genome. In particular, two developments have led to much speculation about the implications of genetic technology for the future of the human species. The first is the Human Genome Project, an international scientific collaboration to identify all 30,000 genes in human DNA. Originally planned to reach completion in 2005, the project has gone faster than anticipated and by 2003 had mapped 99 per cent of it, at what is claimed to be a high degree of accuracy. Shrouded in controversy about the patenting of human genes, the project promises to initiate new possibilities in the treatment of disease. One possible direction this may take is 'pharmacogenetics', which aims to use knowledge about differences in genetic make-up in order to tailor drugs to the way individual metabolisms work. Another direction is 'gene therapy', which aims to alter the way a person's genes are expressed, promising beneficial effects when a 'faulty' or problematic gene causes health problems. In one form of this, new genetic material is introduced into ordinary body cells but is not passed on to future generations. This is at a very early stage of development and faces a number of technical obstacles – but it is being actively pursued. Patient groups representing those with diseases that are currently incurable are actively lobbying for this work to be taken forward and even being tried out. In some cases it has failed and led to the death of patients. However, two French babies with severe immune deficiency disease have (at the time of writing) been successfully treated by supplying them with a normal copy of the gene that causes their illness.

In another form, 'germ line therapy', changes are made to the sperm or ova and these are passed on to future generations. Although this is not currently being investigated in humans, and would have to overcome many technical difficulties and hazards, its possibility at some time in the future clearly has important implications. It would be a form of genetic engineering, holding out the possibility of moulding children's genetic make-up, presumably in the belief that this would determine or enhance their talents and life course. Much moral dismay is evinced at the prospect of 'designer babies' but, as Dingwall (2002: 175–7) argues, even when taking the objections to weak eugenics argued by Shakespeare (see p. 130), the grounds for opposition do not, at the moment, appear to be very clear-cut. As he comments:

> The designed babies of *Brave New World* are the products of an authoritarian society that believes itself to be benign ... However, babies might also be designed by consumer choices in a market. Does

opposition to the first run the risk of creating an illiberal obstacle to the second?

(Dingwall, 2002: 177)

This brings us to the second big development, which is that of cloning. This consists of creating an exact genetic copy of a cell, plant or animal. It is not a new technology. The familiar horticultural technique of taking cuttings produces a clone of the plant in question. Animal cloning has been part of science for several decades but 'Dolly the Sheep' was an important breakthrough, the result of a technique called nuclear transplantation cloning. It involves removing the nucleus of an animal egg cell, which contains its DNA, and replacing it with DNA from another individual. Earlier attempts at this had been successful only when using stem cells – the young, undifferentiated cells found in an embryo – as the replacement material. Dolly, however, was produced not from a stem cell but from DNA taken from a mature adult sheep cell. The result was a sheep with an almost identical genetic constitution to its parent. Although there have been objections to animal cloning per se, it is on the prospect of human cloning that most public discussion has concentrated. Surveys of public opinion in the UK (where human cloning is illegal) and the US (where there is a ban on the use of public research funding for human cloning and the prospect of this being extended to private funded research) show that it is strongly against reproductive human cloning – that is the creation of a whole, living human being who, like Dolly, would be an almost exact copy of one parent. However, public opinion is much more ready to consider therapeutic cloning which would produce specific body parts, for example those used in transplant surgery (Wellcome Trust, 1998).

One reason that Dolly provoked a debate about human rather than animal cloning was that her creation using adult-derived DNA indicated that it was possible to avoid the use of embryos produced specifically for the 'harvesting' of their stem cells. It thus spoke to one of the ethical objections that have been mounted against other reproductive technologies, such as *in vitro* fertilization, because they involve the growth and destruction of human embryos for instrumental use. This highlights the way that the public debate on human cloning has been carried on in almost entirely ethical terms. The debate consists of a series of moral speculations for and against the practice. De Melo-Martin (2002) summarizes the main arguments against cloning as follows: it risks physical harm to the clone; it risks psychological harm to the clone; it will harm society by confusing kinship categories and reducing respect for human life because clones will be seen as replaceable and will be valued as a way of having children with specified characteristics. She summarizes the arguments for cloning as follows: it will help infertile couples; it will overcome genetically transmitted disease; it will allow individuals to clone loved ones who have died.

De Melo–Martin explores these arguments, finding them all faulty because they either take for granted customary but questionable beliefs or they ignore the context within which cloning takes place. So, for example, the argument against cloning on the grounds of psychological risk to the clone (because they would not have a unique identity) assumes that identity is determined by genetic inheritance, thus ignoring the role of upbringing and environment, and discounts the experience of identical twins who do develop unique identities, even though they share their genetic constitution. An example from the other side of the debate is that arguments for cloning on the grounds that it will help infertile couples ignore the fact that there are other less problematic methods of treating infertility and that these should be prioritized when allocating scarce resources.

This kind of moral argumentation proceeds by examining whether or not particular arguments are valid or not. While this is a useful and necessary debate, it tells us very little about whether human cloning is likely to occur and with what consequences. From this point of view it is necessary to look beyond the moral debate for, although moral positions can become associated with social forces, the direction, pace and outcome of societal change are much more likely to be shaped by interests, powers, the balance of forces and the struggle between them. De Melo–Martin's argument that the social context must be taken into account when thinking about human cloning is an important one but when considered from this point of view is double edged. My assessment, for what it is worth and no doubt others will differ, is that it makes it more likely that, at some stage in the not-too-distant future, human cloning will occur (if it has not already done so). This seems more likely than the technology being put aside in a self-denying ordinance. My reasons for believing this are threefold. First, cloning and germ-line therapy research are integrated with other related scientific work. They are not separate fields sealed off from other areas of knowledge. Research on cloning and germ-line engineering in animals and plants will continue, techniques will improve, understanding will increase and the risks are likely to diminish. These developments will be allied with developments in genetic medicine and genomics more generally in such a way that it will become easier for scientists to gain their social acceptance. Second, the market for genetic techniques will develop and will, sooner or later, include cloning. The market will not be dependent on moral approval nor will it depend upon a societal calculation of cost–benefit or a rational calculation of priorities. It will be formed within circuits of supply and demand, that is by the existence of those with the resources to pay for the benefits they feel (however irrationally) it will bring them and which they will not deny themselves. Third, this will occur whether or not there are regulatory frameworks in existence. In a globalizing world it is likely that there will be places where experimentation will be allowed. In any case, as with illegal abortion for sex selection, there will be people ready to break the law. There are already scientists who have declared themselves ready to attempt human cloning.

Although there will always be those who object to cloning and other genetic techniques, these objections are likely to reduce. Previous reproductive technologies, such as IVF, have initially met with strong moral objections and widespread suspicion. These have, however, reduced over time and such a trend is already apparent in the case of cloning. Although we are currently experiencing a rising tide of genetic determinist thinking, much of it is actually mistaken. Many fears about cloning are based on the ill-informed assumption that biology is destiny. Identical twins, for example, develop their own identity because human development is a complex process involving many elements that interact in unpredictable ways. The experience of IVF children who, like clones, are genetically related to only one of their parents, suggests that while curious about their genetic background and eager to know more, this does not damage their relationship with the parents who brought them up. Indeed, their position is very similar to that of adopted children − except that currently, in the UK, IVF children are denied the opportunity to find out more about their biological background while adopted children are not (Feast, 2003).

Nor are human kinship systems as rigid as opponents of cloning suggest. As the anthropological documentation shows, kinship attributions are remarkably flexible and varied (Carsten, 2000). As discussed in Chapter 1, kinship relationships in Euro-American societies have already become unsettled and complicated through new demographic patterns of divorce and remarriage without producing insuperable problems of identity. Reproductive technologies are introducing new instabilities into habitual categories of thought such that the 'natural' basis of reproduction and kinship is being 'defamiliarized' (Franklin and Ragone, 1998) and opened up to choice (Strathern, 1992). As Franklin (1997: 212) tellingly points out, advances in reproductive technology led to the UK parliament, when it was formulating the legislation under which these technologies would be legally regulated, spending many hours debating the meaning of previously taken-for-granted terms like 'mother', 'father', 'conception' and 'fertilization'. She might also have added the term 'child'. For what reproductive technologies do is unsettle the modernist relationship between culture and nature by creating a two-way traffic of mediating connections between the two. Couples who wish for a child can be 'assisted' by technology and in the process nature is 'assisted' by human intervention. More broadly:

> We are already 'post' the modernist model of cosanguinity: it has been geneticised, technologised, instrumentalised, commodified and informationalised and reproduced as virtual sequence data alongside the genomes of mice, dogs, worms, yeasts and fruitflies. Neither can science be assumed to be extra-cultural any longer. Likewise 'kinship' can no

longer be defined as a question of 'natural', 'biological', or 'reproductive' facts, as these criteria are no longer 'given' in the context of , say,
paternity disputes over artificial life forms . . . This will continue to
expand in social, cultural, political, economic and moral significance as
cosanguinity becomes increasingly geneticised, medicalised and instru-
mentalised. Much as forms of human connection may continue to be
naturalised, the simple determination of 'natural facts' and traditional
models of conception are already outdated in such a context.

(Franklin, 1997: 213–14)

The mere prospect of cloning, however far away in time that might be,
makes it possible to imagine and re-imagine a set of ambiguous kinship relations within which someone may simultaneously be the child and the twin
of their parent. However repugnant that prospect may be it is now one
with which we have, if only in our imaginations, to come to terms.

Children and psychopharmaceuticals

It is difficult to estimate how long it will be before human cloning or germ-
line engineering become technically possible. The latter is probably further
away than the former but it would in any case seem wise to start considering the implications of both possibilities. The apparently dramatic
character of these reproductive and genetic technologies should not,
however, be allowed to draw attention away from more immediately
present but rather more mundane issues about childhood. One of these is
the rapid expansion in recent years of a range of psychopharmaceutical
substances, that is drugs with mind- and behaviour-altering properties.

The increased use of such drugs in general among children has been
widely observed. At the moment, however, the debate is largely focused
on the prescription of a variety of drugs to children who are diagnosed
with a condition known as Attention Deficit Hyperactivity Disorder
(ADHD or AD/HD, see p. 137). These prescriptions are mainly of different
central nervous stimulants, including methylphenidate, dextroamphetamine
and amphetamine (all sold under different brand names by competing
pharmaceutical companies). Internationally this has seen a sharp rise all
through the 1990s but the increase in its use has been especially sharp in
the US. According to the US Drug Enforcement Agency methylphenidate
production rose from 1,768 kilograms in 1990 to over 14,957 in 2000. Over
the same time period amphetamine production rose from 417 to 9,007 kilograms (Frontline, 2003a). By the end of the 1990s methylphenidate
prescriptions had risen to approximately 11 million per year and those for
amphetamine to nearly 6 million (Frontline, 2003a). The vast majority of
prescriptions for these drugs in the US are for children diagnosed with
ADHD. According to the United Nations the worldwide trend in the
prescription of these drugs to children is also rising, although not as fast as

in the US. In the UK information on their prescription is protected by commercial secrecy (Lloyd and Norris, 1999) but it is known to show a marked increase over the 1990s. It has been estimated that if US prescribing patterns were replicated in the UK then one in twenty-five children would be taking this type of medication (Prior, 1997).

ADHD is controversial, attracting critics and enthusiasts in equal measure. Broadly speaking it is a disease label given to children whom, it is judged, display inappropriate levels of attention and impulsiveness and/or hyperactivity. It is applied much more to boys than to girls. Often the diagnosis is given when a child has displayed some more or less persistent problem in relation to schoolwork, usually noticed by a parent or teacher, or both, who refer the child to a medical doctor, sometimes after trying other strategies to tackle the perceived problem. Often children diagnosed as ADHD are experienced as under-performing, difficult to deal with and disruptive.

In the US the most commonly used reference work is the Diagnostic and Statistical Manual of Mental Disorders (DSM) published by the American Psychiatric Association (1994) which names, classifies and provides diagnostic criteria for mental illnesses. ADHD has, however, its own history of instability. Something like it first appeared in 1980 as Attention Deficit Disorder (ADD). This shifted the emphasis from terms like 'hyperactivity', which had dominated previous classificatory and diagnostic schemes, replacing it with lack of ability to pay attention. In 1987 a new nomenclature, AD/HD, added hyperactivity back into the picture so that children with or without hyperactivity could be diagnosed as having ADHD. By the end of the 1990s a new emphasis has begun to emerge as a leading biomedical researcher (Barkley, 1997) began to redefine the core problem of ADHD as one of 'self control'. Many believe that this will lead to yet another shift in name and/or diagnostic criteria.

Throughout this book I have argued that dichotomous opposition, for example between the social and the biological, is not helpful in understanding contemporary childhood. However, this kind of thinking pervades how ADHD is understood. For some, ADHD is a biological phenomenon. Biomedically oriented researchers (American Psychiatric Association, 1994; Barkley, 1998) and their lay supporters (see, for example, Children and Adults with Attention Deficit/Hyperactivity Disorder, 2003) argue that underlying changes in nomenclature and diagnostic criteria is an objective, biological condition. It is, they argue, a brain disorder for which no cause has yet been found but which is observable through the behaviour of children (and sometimes adults too, because many argue that ADHD is a lifelong condition). In the biological view, changes in disease classification are merely surface phenomena. One problem with this approach is that it underestimates how discourse constitutes reality and the effects that this can have. So, for example, Baumgaertel *et al.* (1995) have shown that changes in the diagnostic criteria for ADHD between 1987 and 1994 supported a 57 per cent increase in the number of children meeting the criteria. Another problem is that the behaviour used to diagnose ADHD is part of a continuum and there is no sharp point of disjuncture between how ADHD children and others act. Having ADHD is a highly variable judgement, a feature clearly shown by large differences in the proportion of children estimated to display the symptoms (between 6 and 10 per cent of boys, for example) and the geographical variation in its distribution. In the US, 2–2.5 per cent of children are diagnosed, in the UK only 1 per cent and markedly fewer than this in other European countries (Singh, 2002).

Ranged against the biological is the social interpretation. This reading of the condition is largely critical of the very category of ADHD and opposed to the prescription of mind-altering and behaviour-modifying drugs to children. One strand of this opposition is based on the anti-psychiatry ideas of the 1960s. According to these, psychiatry is a form of social control, a way of managing and marginalizing deviant behaviour by medicalizing it (Szasz, 1961). Following this Shrag and Divoky (1975) argue that 'hyperactivity' is a 'myth'. There is, they suggest, no biological condition underlying it, just a set of behaviours which are given a deviant diagnostic label, effectively being a punishment in the form of medication and means by which teachers, parents and other adults can exculpate themselves for the behaviour of their children. Such discourses tend, therefore, to oppose drug prescription on the grounds that it deflects attention from the 'real' social causes of children's problematic behaviour, which are seen in factors such as poor parenting and inadequate or inflexible schooling thus making great play of the social and cultural context of ADHD. However, these arguments are problematic. First, they sometimes deploy a general rhetoric against 'medicating kids', which is hard to sustain because giving medicine to children is an everyday occurrence and it would be unacceptable in many circumstances if drug treatments known to be safe and effective were refused to children who could benefit from them. Second, anti-psychiatry arguments, although making a useful challenge to the medicalization of behaviour, draw too sharp a line between mental and physical illness. For example, while Szasz dismisses diagnoses of mental illness as myths in the service of social control, he seems to accept that diagnoses of physical illness do refer to some underlying biological condition. In fact, the diagnosis of physical conditions is also surrounded by great cultural variability, involves the objectification of subjective states and can be seen to have elements of social control. Szasz's approach tends, therefore, to deny not the concept of mental illness but illness per se. More usefully, Conrad (1975) argues that medicalization occurs under certain conditions. These are when: behaviours that come to be identified as deviant cannot be well controlled by traditional means; the behaviours can plausibly be associated with a biological condition; a treatment such as a pharmaceutical product exists; and the medical profession claims the area as part of its jurisdiction. All of these can be seen in the case of ADHD.

Although this is not Conrad's point, I want to argue that the conditions he specifies contribute to an account of ADHD that allows it to be seen as *both* biological and social. This is possible if it is seen as a heterogeneous assemblage produced through the networks of society, technology and biology. The outline of such a position would contain a number of elements. First, the ability to pay attention, control impulses and sit still varies, because of biological differences in brain functioning between individual children. Second, these differences have no meaning in themselves but take on meaning according to historical and social circumstances. Hyperkinesis, and later ADHD, are products of individual biological differences meeting the demands of mass, compulsory schooling. Schooling, or at least the forms of it that predominate in systems of mass compulsory schooling, require children to sit still, concentrate on tasks and achieve results. Furthermore such schools institute systems of surveillance over large numbers of children, setting up formal and informal systems of comparison and competition. Children are systematically ranked and those who fail to meet the requirements become defined problematic. This is not just a matter of rhetoric but of felt, subjective experience. Teachers, for example, may find it beyond their means to deal with children in the traditional ways allowed by school. Parents who feel their child is failing, and that this will have serious consequences for them, seek remedies, often trying a number of different approaches before accepting the ADHD diagnosis. Other children, too, may find inattentive and impulsive behaviour disruptive of their schooling and children perceived as failing and/or problematic may come to experience themselves in these terms and want to find a solution. These different interests are drawn together, and allied to those of medical scientists, researchers and pharmaceutical companies, by groups such as Children and Adults with Attention Deficit/Hyperactivity Disorder (2003).

The diagnosis of ADHD and subsequent drug treatment thus has an appeal to many different interests. This includes many children diagnosed as ADHD who receive and accept (indeed self-administer) drug treatments. Many children may choose to take drug treatments because they find it beneficial and in fact drug treatments often 'work', though not because the mechanism by which they act is understood. In fact in biomedical terms ADHD is not at all well understood and the drugs used to treat it 'work' because they would create a higher capacity for paying attention whoever took them. They are the same drugs used, for example, by air traffic control personnel during the Second World War precisely because they were found to increase concentration among those carrying out a high-stress but critical task. It is, in part, for this reason that pharmaceutical companies can plausibly claim to be presenting a 'solution' to a problem. This is not to say that they are not motivated by the profits that are to be made in what is a highly lucrative business. Indeed, drug companies spend a great deal of money in promoting their own variant of such drug treatments. They do this by persuading doctors to prescribe their drugs, by having active media strategies to raise the profile of ADHD and by funding self-help groups of parents and children (Lloyd and Norris, 1999).

The sharp rise in the diagnosis of ADHD coincides with the increased pressure on education systems to deliver defined standards of achievement by children. The 1990s also saw an increased level of rhetoric about the responsibility of parents for the well-being of their children. In these circumstances teachers, parents and children can all feel the benefit of the exculpation effect that a medical diagnosis involves. In addition when ADHD became officially classified as a disability, as in effect it has in both the UK and the US, this brought material benefits. Schools became mandated to claim and provide more resources to the affected children. Crucially, drug treatments for ADHD can be argued for in terms of 'levelling the playing field' of school competition. A parent responding to a US Public Service Broadcast documentary wrote in exactly such terms:

> Parents of children with ADHD don't have time for this old Ritalin debate. They know that medications can even the field for their children and give them an equal chance to succeed or fail along with their peers. And that chance is all mothers and fathers really want for their child with ADHD . . . a fair shot at life.
>
> (Frontline, 2003b)

Children in the US and the UK grow up in societies where drug use is pervasive. High-profile stories about athletes who use performance-enhancing drugs are common. The race between those designing and those trying to test for such substances are widely discussed. The use of psychoactive drugs such as Prozac is common and the search for new ones is a growth area among pharmaceutical companies. We can thus see that the 'child-enhancing drug' assemblage serves some interests, producing a self-propelling, multiply-driven phenomenon. At the same time it cuts across and comes into conflict with other interests that wish to limit the availability of such supplements to children. Like opposition to drug use in competitive sports, this mobilizes a rhetoric of 'natural' ability, though in reality such natural abilities are already the product of multiple, but normalized and accepted supplements (like parental help with doing homework or differential access to information on the internet.) Because new types of neuropharmaceuticals are currently being developed, the amphetamine derivatives used to treat ADHD are likely to be only the first of a sequence of such substances. These will proliferate the ambiguity that is generated in the case of ADHD by continually presenting new issues about where the boundary of their acceptability should be drawn, leading to new concatenations of interest and power.

Conclusion

In this chapter I have discussed the ways in which childhood and child-related phenomena are formed as assemblages of heterogeneous materials. In particular I have argued that technology is formed from, and in turn intermingles with, the biological and social. In order to understand this it is important to move away from the idea of a determinant process in which one entity, biological, social or technological drives this process. While the properties of nature and culture are not infinitely malleable, they are over-determined, in the sense that they are complex, emergent and open to contingency. In fact, the entities that we call 'biological', 'technological' and 'social' are already networked together. The processes that occur between them have the rhizomic character that Deleuze and Guattari write about. This means that the effects that are created by their interweaving create new assemblages, possibilities and problems in a non-teleological process. This is apparent right across the scale, from the everyday micro processes examined by Ogilvie-Whyte to the global scale of information and communication technologies.

Seen in this perspective the three technologies that I have discussed can each be seen as extending and supplementing childhood in ways that destabilize various taken-for-granted oppositions and boundaries. The controversial character of the psychopharmaceuticals used with children derives from the way in which they blur the distinction between drugs which treat and those that enhance performance. Schooling in rich countries is a central means by which children are sorted and distributed into the system of social rewards. In this highly competitive setting the enhancement of performance is bound to create a clash of interests for and against their use – just as it does in competitive sport. A new boundary is being negotiated about the legitimacy of supplementing children's performance at school (and perhaps in wider arenas too). ICTs destabilize the boundary between the public and the private spheres, and between adulthood and childhood. They help to create conditions in which the dependency of children becomes problematic and in which the voices of minorities, including children, might be constructed and amplified. Reproductive technologies are destabilizing the taken-for-granted assumptions about how human life is brought into being and how to reckon the basis of related-ness between children and parents, thus destabilizing the 'natural' order of the generations. I am not suggesting the examples I have used identify the factors that will necessarily shape the future of childhood. What will be important to its shaping remains to be seen and it may turn out to be phenomena quite different from the ones I have discussed. They do, however, provide instances of the assemblages of culture and nature, of society and technology, and of discourse and materiality to which those studying childhood must give their attention if we are even to begin to understand the trajectories that childhood will take.

Afterword

An important implication of my argument is that childhood studies, a field that has been emerging for well over a century, may now be able to find a conceptual apparatus for overcoming the narrow and fragmenting disciplinary gaze through which childhood has been seen for over a century. Where previously there was a collection of more or less incommensurable discourses between the natural sciences, the social sciences and the humanities, it is possible to see how a more coherent (though not necessarily unified) field of enquiry might emerge. The last part of the twentieth century saw an erosion of the boundaries between many categories that in modernist thought had been seen as mutually exclusive. This gave rise to a new fluidity in ontological assumptions, such that, for example, the distinction between the human and the non-human could be treated as shifting and negotiable rather than fixed and given. Theoretical and conceptual languages, such as those drawn on throughout this book, have emerged that can speak across oppositional dualisms, including the distinction between nature and culture, without reducing one to the other or creating a priori relations of dominance between them. It remains to be seen how successful this effort will be and where it will lead but I have little doubt that childhood studies should join in, draw from and contribute to it. Through this process childhood studies might gather the potential to be a genuinely interdisciplinary field.

The effort to create such a field will, in my view, be most effective if it is part of a wider effort to move beyond dualistic thinking in general. The a priori division of the world into mutually exclusive entities betrays an unwillingness to look beyond appearances to understand how such divisions are made, come into being and fade away. What could be the object of understanding (that is how differences arises) is thus reconstituted as a taken-for-granted template for understanding the world. So, for example, the distinction between being and becoming has been used to draw a line between the concerns of the sociology of childhood, which wishes (for good reasons) to see children as beings, and those of developmental psychology, which (again with good reason) wishes to see children as becomings. This leads into a self-defeating loop in which the very conditions of children's lives, their culture–natures and their being–becomings, are split and denied. If the way forward for childhood studies that I advocate in this book is to be productive, it requires some re-conceptualization of childhood's ontology. Childhood should be seen as neither 'natural' nor 'cultural' but a multiplicity of 'nature–cultures', that is a variety of complex hybrids constituted from heterogeneous materials and emergent through time. It is cultural, biological, social, individual, historical, technological, spatial, material, discursive . . . and more. Childhood is not seen as a unitary phenomenon but a multiple set of constructions emergent from the connection and disconnection, fusion and separation of these heterogeneous materials. Each particular construction, and these come in scales running from the individual child to historically constituted forms of childhood, have a non-linear history, a being in becoming that is open-ended and non-teleological.

The methodology adequate to childhood thought of in this way would not reduce it to any of its particular, separated-out aspects. It requires a non-reductionist approach, even as it is recognized that the materials going into its construction are not easily separable from each other. Such an idea of childhood studies would defy oppositional dualisms, being practised through non-dualist modes of thought that are concerned not to accept oppositions but problematize them by examining the gradients from which they are produced. It would, therefore, be concerned to trace the connections and mediations through which childhood comes into being. Such analysis requires a symmetrical approach, one that is ecumenical in regarding both the human and the non-human as potentially important, making no a priori assumptions about what is determinant but leaving this open to empirical enquiry. Instances of childhood would, therefore, be understood as empirical effects of an open-ended process in which the different elements through which they are constructed have come into play.

Once stated in this way it becomes obvious that the same approach could be used in the study of adulthood. There is, in this sense, no difference in principle between understanding childhood and adulthood. So while the relational approach involves seeing how childhood is constituted in relation to adulthood, as the idea of generational relations and the life course both imply, the relationality of childhood cannot be confined to either of these. Generational relations and life courses are constructed through their partial dependence and connection with a multitude of different entities. Again, it becomes necessary to trace the heterogeneous networks within which they are constructed. This argument implies that, alongside other oppositional dualisms, the distinction between childhood and adulthood is not itself taken-for-granted. Rather it should be problematized and the attempt made to understand how and why the distinction arises, what the materials and processes are that construct it and how its shifting boundaries are constituted and reconstituted.

One immediate, practical implication of my argument is the need to intensify the interdisciplinarity of childhood studies. The social study of childhood is already significantly multi-disciplinary, with contributors from across the social sciences and humanities. There are, however, areas where interdisciplinary dialogue is weak. One such area is that between sociology and psychology, which was in some respects a discipline against which the new social study of childhood constituted itself: children as individuals versus children as social. Sustaining this picture depended upon clinging to some rather crude stereotypes of both sociology's and psychology's engagement with childhood. The new sociology of childhood has been particularly prone to this, even though it is clear that many psychologists are concerned with similar issues. Examples include the work of Woodhead (1999) in the UK, Cole (1997) in the US, Goodnow *et al.* (1995) in Australia and Haavind (2004, in press) in Norway. The Vygotskian tradition of developmental psychology is both socially and historically aware and grounded in a materialist approach. Its recent development as 'activity theory', which explicitly recognizes the role of material artefacts is similar in many respects to actor–network theory and is compatible with the discussion of the relationship between childhood and various socio-bio-technical assemblages found in the last chapter of this book. More dialogue that explores common ground as well as differences could be useful here.

I am also acutely aware that the version of interdisciplinarity presented in this book is a selective one. It reflects my own academic training, which has been, at various points, in the natural sciences, sociology, history and anthropology. My discussion is far too neglectful of most of the humanities, even though I am sure that, to name but just a few, aesthetics, art history, literary criticism and media studies, all have something very valuable to contribute. However, this realization also underlines that interdisciplinarity does not entail becoming an expert in everything. Looking into other disciplines runs the risk of dilettantism and amateurism and I may well be guilty of either or both of these, a matter that I leave others to judge. But even if I am to be found at fault in the accuracy with which I have borrowed or translated from other disciplines, I am unrepentant. I think it is worth the risk if doing so stimulates the imagination and, especially, if it opens new lines of thinking – even if these might be better pursued by others more expert than I.

The call for interdisciplinarity is, of course, frequently heard in contemporary academic life, at least as a rhetoric. Its potential advantages are well known. It can lead to more creative work than is likely within a single discipline. The cross-disciplinary gaze is more likely to detect and correct the naive assumptions to which monodisciplinary work is vulnerable. However, even if there is agreement that childhood studies should move towards interdisciplinarity, it is far from clear how this should be accomplished. Woodhead (2003) recently set out three possible pathways that childhood studies might follow in the pursuit of interdisciplinarity. These are:

A 'clearinghouse model' would encompass all studies of children and childhood, all research questions, methodologies and disciplinary approaches.

A 'pick 'n mix model' would be more selective but still incorporate a wide range of approaches. The selection criteria might be about the specific topics studied or orientation to the field.

A 're-branding model' might appear to have interdisciplinary aspirations but would mainly be about redefining a traditional field of enquiry while still adhering to conventional disciplinary boundaries.

(Woodhead, 2003: section 3.1)

Like Woodhead, I do not know whether these are the only possibilities or, from among them, which is the most promising, realistic or wise. However, I do agree with his caution against abandoning disciplinary-based studies. Interdisciplinarity does not imply non-disciplinarity but rather traffic between two or more disciplines. Childhood studies could, for the moment, constitute themselves as a meeting place of the disciplines, a process that might encourage the patience, open-mindedness and the capacity to step out of disciplinary comfort zones that the longer-term aim of interdisciplinarity requires. It is towards this process that this book is intended to make a contribution.

References

Alanen, L. (2001a) 'Explorations in Generational Analysis', in Alanen, L. and Mayall, B. (eds), *Conceptualizing Child–Adult Relations*, London: Falmer.

Alanen, L. (2001b) 'Childhood as a Generational Condition: Children's Daily Life in a Central Finland Town', in Alanen, L. and Mayall, B. (eds), *Conceptualizing Child–Adult Relations*, London: Falmer.

Alderson, P. (1993) *Children's Consent to Surgery*, Buckingham: Open University Press.

American Psychiatric Association (1994) *Diagnostic and Statistical Manual of Mental Disorders* (4th edn), Washington, DC: APA.

Archard, D. (1993) *Children: Rights and Childhood*, London: Routledge.

Aries, P. (1962) *Centuries of Childhood: A Social History of Family Life*, London: Jonathan Cape.

Armstrong, D. (1983) *Political Anatomy of the Body: Medical Knowledge in Britain in the Twentieth Century*, Cambridge: Cambridge University Press.

Armstrong, D. (1987) 'Bodies of Knowledge: Foucault and the Problem of Human Anatomy', in Scambler, G. (ed.), *Sociological Theory and Medical Sociology*, London: Tavistock.

Barker, M. (ed.) (1984) *The Video Nasties: Freedom and Censorship in the Media*, London: Methuen.

Barkley, R.A. (1997) *ADHD and the Nature of Self-Control*, New Jersey: Guilford Press.

Barkley, R.A. (1998) *Attention Deficit Hyperactivity Disorders: A Handbook for Diagnosis and Treatment*, New York: Guilford Press.

Bauman, Z. (1991) *Modernity and Ambivalence*, Cambridge: Polity Press.

Baumgaertel, A., Wolraich, M. and Dietrich, M. (1995) 'Comparison of Diagnostic Criteria for Attention Deficit Disorders in a German Elementary School Sample', *Journal of the Academy of Child and Adolescent Psychiatry*, 34: 629–38.

Beck, U. (1992) *Risk Society: Towards a New Modernity*, London: Sage.

Beck, U. (1998) *Democracy Without Enemies*, Cambridge: Polity Press.

Bijker, W. and Law, J. (eds) (1994) *Shaping Technology/Building Society: Studies in Sociotechnical Change*, Cambridge, MA: MIT Press.

Bingham, N., Valentine, G. and Holloway, S.L. (1999) 'Where Do You Want to Go Tomorrow? Connecting Children and the Internet', *Environment and Planning*, 17: 655–72.

Birch, H.G. and Dye, J. (1970) *Disadvantaged Children: Health, Nutrition and School Failure*, New York: Grune & Stratton.

Bluebond-Langner, M., Perkel, D. and Goertzel, T. (1991) 'Paediatric Cancer Patients' Peer Relationships: The Impact of an Oncology Camp Experience', *Journal of Psychosocial Oncology*, 9 (2): 67–80.

Bobbio, N. (1996) *Left And Right: The Significance of a Political Distinction*, Cambridge: Polity Press.

Bogerhoff Mulder, M. (1998) 'The Demographic Transition: Are We Any Closer to an Evolutionary Explanation?', *Trends in Ecology and Evolution*, 13: 266–70.

Bogin, B. (1998) 'Evolutionary and Biological Aspects of Childhood', in Panter-Brick, C. (ed.), *Biosocial Perspectives on Children*, Cambridge: Cambridge University Press.

Boyden, J. (1997) 'Childhood and the Policy Makers', in James, A. and Prout, A. (eds), *Constructing and Reconstructing Childhood: Contemporary Issues in the Sociological Study of Childhood* (2nd edn), London: Falmer Press.

Boyden, J., Ling, B. and Myers, W. (1998) *What Works for Working Children?*, Stockholm: Radda Barnen/UNICEF.

Bradshaw, J. (2000) 'Child Poverty in Comparative Perspective', in Gordon, D. and Townsend, P. (eds), *Breadline Europe: The Measurement of Poverty*, Bristol: Policy Press.

Bradshaw, J. (ed.) (2001) *Poverty: The Outcomes for Children*, London: Family Policy Studies Centre.

Bronfenbrenner, E. (1979) *The Ecology of Human Development: Experiments by Nature and Design*, Cambridge, MA: Harvard University Press.

Brown, A. (2000) *The Darwin Wars: The Scientific Battle for the Soul of Man*, New York: Simon & Schuster.

Buckingham, D. (2000) *After the Death of Childhood: Growing Up in the Age of the Electronic Media*, Cambridge: Polity Press.

Buss, D.M. (1994) *The Evolution of Desire: Strategies of Human Mating*, New York: Basic Books.

Buss, D.M. (1999) *Evolutionary Psychology: The New Science of the Mind*, London: Allyn & Bacon.

Buti, A. (2002) 'British Child Migration to Australia: History, Senate Inquiry and Responsibilities', *E Law – Murdoch University Electronic Journal of Law*, 9: 4, www. murdoch.edu.au/elaw/issues/v9n4/buti94_text.html, accessed 2 November 2002.

Byrne, D. (1998) *Complexity Theory and the Social Sciences*, London: Routledge.

Callon, M. (1986) 'Some Elements of a Sociology of Translation: Domestication of the Scallops and the Fishermen of St Briuec Bay', in Law, J. (ed.), *Power, Action and Belief: A New Sociology of Knowledge?*, London: Routledge & Kegan Paul.

Callon, M. and Latour, B. (1981) 'Unscrewing the Big Leviathan: How Actors Macro-Structure Reality and How Sociologists Help Them', in Knorr-Cetina, K. and Cicourel, A. (eds), *Towards an Integration of Micro and Macrosociologies*, London: Routledge & Kegan Paul.

Carsten, J. (2000) *Cultures of Relatedness: New Approaches to the Study of Kinship*, Cambridge: Cambridge University Press.

Castells, M. (2000) *The Rise of the Network Society, Volumes 1–3*, Oxford: Blackwell.

Chernin, K. (1983) *Womansize: The Tyranny of Slenderness*, London: The Women's Press.

Children and Adults with Attention Deficit/Hyperactivity Disorder (2003), web pages at www.chadd.org/index.cfm, accessed 15 December, 2003.

Children and Young People's Unit (2000) *Tomorrow's Future: Building a Strategy for Children and Young People*, London: Children and Young People's Unit.

Christensen, P. (1994) 'Children as the Cultural Other', *KEA: Zeischrift für Kultur-wissenschaften, TEMA: Kinderwelten,* 6: 1–16.

Christensen, P. (1999) 'Towards an Anthropology of Childhood Sickness: An Ethnographic Study of Danish School Children', Ph D. thesis, University of Hull

Christensen, P. (2000) 'Childhood and the Construction of the Vulnerable Body', in Prout, A. (ed.), *The Body, Childhood and Society,* London: Macmillan.

Christensen, P. (2002) 'Why more "Quality Time" is Not on the Top of Children's Lists', *Children and Society,* 16: 1–12.

Christensen, P. (2003) 'Børn, mad og daglige rutiner', *Barn.* Tema: Barn og mat. Smakebiter fra Aktuell Forskning. nr. 2–3: 119–35. Norsk Senter for Barne-forskning.

Christensen, P. and Prout, A. (2004, forthcoming) 'Anthropological and Sociological Perspectives on the Study of Children', in Greene, S. and Hogan, D. (eds), *Research-ing Children,* London: Sage.

Christensen, P., James, A. and Jenks, C. (2000) 'Home and Movement: Children Constructing Family Time', in Holloway, S. and Valentine, G. (eds), *Children's Geographies: Living, Playing and Transforming Everyday Worlds,* London: Routledge.

Clarke, L. (1996) 'Demographic Change and the Family Situation of Children', in Brannen, J. and O'Brien, M. (eds), *Children in Families: Research and Policy,* London: Falmer Press.

Cole, M. (1997) *Cultural Psychology: A Once and Future Discipline,* Cambridge, MA: Harvard University Press.

Cole, M. (1998) 'Culture in Development', in Woodhead, M., Faulkner, D. and Littleton, K. (eds), *Cultural Worlds of Early Childhood,* London: Routledge.

Commission of the European Community (2001) 'Communication from the Com-mission to the Council, the European Parliament, the Economic and Social Committee and the Committee of the Regions. Draft joint report on social inclu-sion. Part I – The European Union', Brussels: European Commission.

Connolly, P. (1998) *Racism, Gender Identities and Young Children,* London: Routledge.

Conrad, P. (1975) 'The Discovery of Hyperkinesis', *Social Problems,* 23: 12–23.

Corea, G., Hanmer, J., Klein, R.D. and Rowland, R. (1985) *Man-Made Women: How New Reproductive Technologies Affect Women,* London: Hutchinson.

Corsaro, W.A. (1996) 'Early Education, Children's Lives and the Transition from Home to School in Italy and the United States', *International Journal of Comparative Sociology,* 37: 121–39.

Corsaro, W.A. (1997) *The Sociology of Childhood,* Thousand Oaks, CA: Pine Forge Press.

Corsten, M. (2003) 'Biographical Revisions and the Coherence of a Generation', in Mayall, B. and Zeiher, H. (eds), *Childhood in Generational Perspective,* London: Institute of Education.

Coward, R. (1989) *The Whole Truth: The Myth of Alternative Health,* London: Faber & Faber.

Creighton, C. (1999) 'The Rise and Decline of the Male Breadwinner Family in Britain', *Cambridge Journal of Economics,* 23: 519–42.

Croissant, J.L. (1998) 'Growing Up Cyborg: Development Stories for Postmodern Children', in Davis-Floyd, R. and Dumit, J. (eds), *Cyborg Babies: From Techno-Sex to Techno-Tots,* London: Routledge.

Cunningham, H. (1991) *The Children of the Poor: Representations of Childhood since the Seventeenth Century,* Oxford: Blackwell.

Cunningham, H. and Viazzo, P.P. (1996) *Child Labour in Historical Perspective 1800–1995*, Florence, UNICEF.

Davie, R., Upton, G. and Varma, V. (eds) (1996) *The Voice of the Child*, London: Falmer Press.

Davis, H. and Bourhill, M. (1997) '"Crisis": The Demonisation of Children and Young People', in Scraton, P. (ed.), *'Childhood' in 'Crisis'?*, London: UCL Press.

Davis-Floyd, R. and Dumit, J. (1998) *Cyborg Babies: From Techno-Sex to Techno-Tots*, New York and London: Routledge.

Dawkins, R. (1976) *The Selfish Gene*, Oxford: Oxford Paperbacks.

De Landa, M. (1997) *A Thousand Years of Nonlinear History*, New York: Zone Books.

Deleuze, G. (1997) *Essays Critical and Clinical*, London: Verso Books.

Deleuze, G. and Guattari, F. (1988) *A Thousand Plateaus: Capitalism and Schizophrenia II*, London: Athlone.

De Melo-Martin, I. (2002) 'On Cloning Human Beings', *Bioethics*, 16 (3): 246–65.

Denis, W. (1972) *Historical Readings in Developmental Psychology*, New York: Appleton-Century-Crofts.

Dickenson, D. (1999) 'Can Children and Young People Consent to Being Tested for Adult Onset Genetic Disorders', *British Medical Journal*, 318: 1063–6.

Dingwall, R. (2002) 'Bioethics', in Pilnick, A., *Genetics and Society: An Introduction*, Buckingham: Open University Press.

Donzelot, J. (1979) *The Policing of Families*, London: Hutchinson.

Dreitzel, H.P. (ed.) (1973) *Childhood and Socialization*, San Francisco: Jossey-Bass.

Ehrenreich, B. and English, D. (1993) *Witches, Midwives and Nurses: A History of Women Healers*, Westbury: Feminist Press.

Elder, G.H., Modell, J. and Parke, R.H. (1993) (eds) *Children in Time and Place*, New York: Cambridge University Press.

Elkind, D. (1981) *The Hurried Child: Growing Up Too Fast Too Soon*, Reading, MA: Addison Wesley.

Esping-Andersen, G. (1990) *The Three Worlds of Welfare Capitalism*, Princeton, NJ: Princeton University Press.

Esping-Andersen, G. (ed.) (1996) *Welfare States in Transition: National Adaptations in Global Economies*, London: Sage.

European Commission (1996) *The Demographic Situation in the European Union – 1995*, Brussels: European Commission.

Eve, R.A., Horsfall, S. and Lee, M.E. (eds) (1997) *Chaos, Complexity and Sociology: Myths, Models and Theories*, London: Sage.

Facer, K., Furlong, R., Furlong, J. and Sutherland, R. (2001a) 'Constructing the Child Computer User: From Public Policy to Private Practice', *British Journal of Sociology of Education*, 22 (1): 91–108.

Facer, K., Furlong, R., Furlong, J. and Sutherland, R. (2001b) 'Home is Where the Hardware Is: Young People, the Domestic Environment and "Access" to New Technologies', in Hutchby, I. and Moran-Ellis, J. (eds), *Children, Technology and Culture: The Impacts of Technology in Children's Everyday Lives*, London: RoutledgeFalmer.

Feast, J. (2003) 'Using and Not Losing the Message from the Adoption Experience for Donor-Assisted Conception', *Human Fertility*, 6: 41–5.

Federal Interagency Forum on Child and Family Statistics (1999) *America's Children: Key National Indicators of Well-being, 1999*, Federal Interagency Forum on Child and Family Statistics, Washington, DC: US Printing Office.

Firestone, S. (1972) *The Dialectics of Sex*, Harmondsworth: Penguin.

Flekkoy, G.D. and Kaufman, N.H. (1997) *The Participation Rights of the Child: Rights and Responsibilities in Family and Society*, London: Jessica Kingsley.

Franklin, B. (1995) *Handbook of Children's Rights: Comparative Policy and Practice*, London: Routledge.

Franklin, S. (1997) *Embodied Progress: A Cultural Account of Assisted Conception*, London: Routledge.

Franklin, S. and Ragone, H. (eds) (1998) 'Introduction', in Franklin, S. and Ragone, H. (eds), *Reproducing Reproduction: Kinship, Power and Technological Innovation*, Philadelphia: University of Pennsylvania Press.

Frønes, I. (1993) 'Changing Childhoods', *Childhood*, 1: 1.

Frønes, I. (1995) *Among Peers: On the Meaning of Peers in the Process of Socialisation*, Oslo: Scandinavian University Press.

Frønes, I. (1997) 'Children of the Post-Industrial Family', Mimeo, Department of Sociology and Human Geography, University of Oslo.

Frontline (2003a) 'Statistics on Stimulant Use', www.pbs.org/wgbh/pages/frontline/shows/medicating/drugs/stats.html, accessed 14 December 2003.

Frontline (2003b) 'Discussion/Share Your Story', www.pbs.org/wgbh/pages/frontline/shows/medicating/talk/, accessed 14 December, 2003.

Fukuyama, F. (2003) *Our Posthuman Future: Consequences of the Biotechnology Revolution*, London: Profile Books.

García Coll, C., Szalacha, L. and Palacios, N. (2004) 'Children of Dominican, Portuguese, and Cambodian Immigrant Families: Academic Attitudes and Pathways During Middle Childhood', in Cooper, C.R., García Coll, C., Bartko, T., Davis, H. and Chatman, C. (eds), *Hills of Gold: Rethinking Diversity and Contexts as Resources for Children's Developmental Pathways*, Mahwah, NJ: Lawrence Erlbaum.

Gibson, K.R. (1993) 'General Introduction: Animal Minds, Human Minds', in Gibson, K.R. and Ingold, T. (eds), *Tools, Language and Cognition in Human Evolution*, Cambridge: Cambridge University Press.

Giddens, A. (1976) *The New Rules of Sociological Method*, London: Hutchinson.

Giddens, A. (1990) *The Consequences of Modernity*, Cambridge: Polity Press.

Giddens, A. (1991) *Modernity and Self-identity*, Cambridge: Polity Press.

Giele, J.Z. and Elder, G.H. (1998) *Methods of Life Course Research*, London: Sage.

Giesecke, H. (1985) *Das Ende der Erziehung*, Stuttgart: Klett-Cotta-Verlag.

Goldstein, D. (1998) 'Nothing Bad Intended: Child Discipline, Punishment, and Survival in a Shantytown in Rio de Janeiro', in Scheper-Hughes, N. and Sargeant, C. (eds), *Small Wars: The Cultural Politics of Childhood*, Berkeley: University of California–Berkeley Press.

Goldstein, H. and Heath, A. (eds) (2000) *Educational Standards* (Proceedings of the British Academy 102), Oxford: Oxford University Press.

Goodnow, J.J., Miller, P.M. and Kessel, F. (eds) (1995) *Cultural Practices as Contexts for Development*, San Francisco: Jossey-Bass.

Gray, R. (1992) 'Death of the Gene: Developmental Systems Strike Back', in Griffiths, P. (ed.), *Trees of Life*, The Hague: Kluwer.

Haavind, H. (2004, in press) 'Contesting annd Recognizing Historical Changes and Selves in Development: Methodological Challenges', in Weisner, T.S. (ed.), *Discovering Successful Pathways in Children's Development: Mixed Methods in the Study of Childhood and Family Life*, Chicago, IL: University of Chicago Press.

Haraway, D.J. (1990) *Primate Visions: Gender, Race, and Nature in the World of Modern Science*, London: Routledge.

Haraway, D.J. (1991) *Simians, Cyborgs and Women: The Reinvention of Nature*, London: Free Association Books.

Hart, R. (1992) *Children's Participation: From Tokenism to Citizenship*, Florence: Innocenti Essays.

Hawkes, T. (1972) *Metaphor*, London: Methuen.

Hemmens, C. and Bennett, K. (1999) 'Juvenile Curfews and the Courts: Judicial Response to a Not-So-New Crime Control Strategy', *Crime and Delinquency*, 45 (1): 99–121.

Hendrick, H. (1997a) *Children, Childhood and English Society 1880–1990*, Cambridge: Cambridge University Press.

Hendrick, H. (1997b) 'Constructions and Reconstructions of British Childhood: An Interpretative Survey, 1800 to the Present', in James, A. and Prout, A., *Constructing and Reconstructing Childhood: Contemporary Issues in the Sociological Study of Childhood* (2nd edn), London: Falmer Press.

Heywood, C. (2001) *A History of Childhood*, Cambridge: Polity Press.

Higonnet, A. (1998) *Pictures of Innocence: The History and Crisis of Ideal Childhood*, London: Thames & Hudson.

Hobcraft, J. (1998) 'Intergenerational and Life-Course Transmission of Social Exclusion: Influences and Childhood Poverty, Family Disruption and Contact with the Police', London: London School of Economic, Centre for the Analysis of Social Exclusion, Paper 15.

Hochschild, A.R. (2001) 'Global Care Chains and Emotional Surplus Value', in Hutton, H. and Giddens, A. (eds), *On the Edge: Living with Global Capitalism*, London: Vintage.

Holden, C. and Mace, R. (1997) 'Phylogenetic Analysis of the Evolution of Lactose Digestion in Adults', *Human Biology*, 69: 605–28.

Holland, J. and Thomson, R. (1999) 'Respect – Youth Values: Identity, Diversity and Social Change', ESRC Children 5–16 Research Programme Briefing, www.esrc.ac.uk/curprog.html, accessed 14 October 2003.

Holland, P. (1992) *What is a Child? Popular Images of Childhood*, London: Virago Press.

Holloway, S.L. and Valentine, G. (2001) 'It's Only as Stupid as You Are: Children and Adults' Negotiations of ICT Competence at Home and at School', *Social and Cultural Geography*, 2 (1): 25–42.

Humanoid Robotics Group, Massachusetts Institute of Technology (2003), www.ai.mit.edu/projects/humanoid-robotics-group/cog/current-projects.html, accessed 6 December 2003.

Illingworth, R. (1986) *The Normal Child: Some Problems of the Early Years and Their Treatment* (9th edn), Edinburgh: Churchill Livingstone.

Ingold, T. (1993) 'Tool Use, Sociality and Intelligence', in Gibson, K.R. and Ingold, T. (eds), *Tools, Language and Cognition in Human Evolution*, Cambridge: Cambridge University Press.

International Labour Office (2003) 'Labour Market Trends and Globalisation's Impact on Them', Geneva: International Labour Office, consulted at www.itcilo.it/english/actrav/telearn/global/ilo/seura/mains.htm on 3 March 2003.

International Obesity Task Force (2003) 'IOTF Obesity in Europe Section Appendix 1', www.iotf.org/, accessed 22 December 2003.

James, A. (2000) 'Embodied Being-(s): Understanding the Self and the Body in Childhood', in Prout, A. (ed.), *The Body, Childhood and Society*, London: Macmillan.

James, A., Jenks, C. and Prout, A. (1998) *Theorizing Childhood*, Cambridge: Polity Press.

Janson, C.H. and Van Schaik, C.P. (2002) 'Ecological Risk Aversion in Juvenile Primates: Slow and Steady Wins the Race', in Pereira, M.E. and Fairbanks, L.A. (eds), *Juvenile Primates: Life History, Development and Behaviour*, Chicago, IL: Chicago University Press.

Jenks, C. (1982) (ed.) *The Sociology of Childhood – Essential Readings*, London: Batsford.

Jenks, C. (1990) *Childhood*, London: Routledge.

Joshi, H., Cooksey, E., Wiggins, R.D., McCulloch, I., Verropoulou, G. and Clarke, L. (1999) 'Diverse Family Living Situations and Child Development: A Multi-Level Analysis Comparing Longitudinal Evidence from Britain and the United States', *International Journal of Law, Policy and the Family*, 13: 292–314.

Katz, J. (1997) *Virtuous Reality*, New York: Random House.

Kehily, M.J. and Swann, J. (eds) (2003) *Children's Cultural Worlds*, Chichester: Wiley and the Open University Press.

Kendrick, A. (1998) *'Who Do We Trust?': The Abuse of Children Living Away from Home in the United Kingdom*, paper presented to the 12th International Congress on Child Abuse and Neglect; Protecting Children: Innovation and Inspiration, ISPCAN – International Society for Prevention of Child Abuse and Neglect, Auckland, 6–9 September.

Kline, S. (1995) *Out of the Garden: Toys and Children's Culture in the Age of TV Marketing*, London: Verso.

Lakoff, G. and Johnson, M. (1980) *Metaphors We Live By*, Chicago, IL: Chicago University Press.

Laland, K.N. and Brown, G.R. (2002) *Sense and Nonsense: Evolutionary Perspectives on Human Behaviour*, Oxford: Oxford University Press.

Lansdown, G. (1995) *Taking Part: Children's Participation in Decision Making*, London: Institute for Public Policy Research.

Lash, S. and Urry, J. (1994) *Economies of Sign and Space*, London: Sage.

Latour, B. (1991) 'Technology is Society Made Durable' in Law, J. (ed), *A Sociology of Monsters*, London: Routledge.

Latour, B. (1993) *We Have Never Been Modern*, Hemel Hempstead: Harvester/Wheatsheaf.

Latour, B., and Woolgar, S. (1986) *Laboratory Life: The Construction of Scientific Facts* (2nd edn), Princeton, NJ: Princeton University Press.

Lavalette, M. (1994) *Child Employment in the Capitalist Labour Market*, Aldershot: Avebury.

Law, J. (1992) 'Notes on the Theory of the Actor-Network: Ordering Strategy and Heterogeneity', *Systems Practice*, 5 (4): 379–93.

Law, J. (1994) *Organising Modernity*, Oxford: Blackwell.

Law, J. and Hassard, J. (1999) *Actor Network Theory and After*, Oxford: Blackwell.

Lee, N. (1999) 'The Challenge of Childhood: The Distribution of Childhood's Ambiguity in Adult Institutions', *Childhood*, 6 (4): 455–74.

Lee, N. (2000) 'Faith in the Body? Childhood, Subjecthood and Sociological Enquiry', in Prout, A. (ed.), *The Body, Childhood and Society*, London: Macmillan.

Lee, N. (2001a) *Childhood and Society: Growing Up in an Age of Uncertainty*, Buckingham: Open University Press.

Lee, N. (2001b) 'The Extensions of Childhood: Technologies, Children and Independence', in Hutchby, I. and Moran-Ellis, J. (eds), *Children, Technology and Culture: The Impacts of Technologies in Children's Everyday Lives*, London: RoutledgeFalmer.

Levin, D. and Rosenquest, B. (2001) 'The Increasing Role of Electronic Toys in the Live of Infants and Toddlers: Should we be Concerned?', *Contemporary Issues in Early Childhood*, 2 (2): 91–120.

Lewin, R. (1993) *Principles of Human Evolution*, Oxford: Blackwell Science.

Lewis, J. (1992) 'Gender and the Development of Welfare Regimes', *Journal of European Social Policy*, 2: 159–73.

Lewontin, R. (2000) *The Triple Helix: Gene, Organism and Environment*, Cambridge, MA: Harvard University Press.

Linney, J.A. (2000) 'Assessing Ecological Constructs and Community Context', in Rappaport, J. and Seidman, E. (eds), *Handbook of Community Psychology*, New York: Kluwer Academic/Plenum Publishers.

Lloyd, G. and Norris, C. (1999) 'Including ADHD?', *Disability and Society*, 14 (4): 505–17.

Lorenz, K. (1970) *Studies in Animal and Human Behaviour*, London: Methuen.

Lumsden, C.J. and Wilson, E.O. (1981) *Genes, Minds and Culture: The Coevolutionary Process*, Cambridge, MA: Harvard University Press.

MacKenzie, D. and Wajcman, J. (eds) (1985) *The Social Shaping of Technology*, Milton Keynes: Open University Press.

Mannheim, K. (1952/1927) 'The Problem of Generations', in Mannheim, K. (ed.), *Essays in the Sociology of Knowledge*, London: Routledge & Kegan Paul.

Mannion, G. and I'Anson, J. (2003) 'New Assemblages within the Arts Fold: Exploring Young People's Subjectification through Self-directed Photography, Photo-journey and Photo-elicitation', *Crossing Boundaries: The Value of Interdisciplinary Research*, Proceedings of the 3rd Conference of the Environmental Psychology UK Network, June.

Martin, E. (1990) 'The Ideology of Reproduction: The Reproduction of Ideology', in Ginsburg, F. and Tsing, A.L. (eds), *Uncertain Terms: Negotiating Gender in American Culture*, Boston: Beacon Press.

Marx, K. and Engels, F. (1848/1968) *Manifesto of the Communist Party*, Moscow: Progress Publishers.

Massey, D.S. (1998) 'March of Folly: US Immigration Policy NAFTA', *The American Prospect*, March–April: 22–3.

Mayall, B. (ed.) (1994) *Children's Childhoods: Observed and Experienced*, London: Falmer.

Maybin, J. and Woodhead, M. (2003) (eds) *Childhood in Context*, Chichester: Wiley and the Open University Press.

Milburn, K. (2000) 'Children, Parents and the Construction of the "Healthy Body" in Middle Class Families', in Prout, A. (ed.), *The Body, Childhood and Society*, London: Macmillan.

Montanari, I. (2000) 'From Family Wage to Marriage Subsidy and Child Benefits: Controversy and Consensus in the Development of Family Support', *Journal of European Social Policy*, 10 (4): 307–33.

Morris, D. (1969) *The Naked Ape*, London: Corgi.

Moss, P., Dillon, J. and Statham, J. (2000) 'The "Child in Need" and "The Rich Child": Discourses, Constructions and Practices', *Critical Social Policy*, 20 (2): 233–54.

Murdoch, G. and McCron, R. (1979) 'The Television and Delinquency Debate', *Screen Education*, 30.

Näsman, E. (1994) 'Individualisation and Institutionalisation of Children', in Qvortrup, J., Bardy, M., Sgritta, G. and Wintersberger, H. (eds), *Childhood Matters: Social Theory, Practice and Politics*, Aldershot: Avebury.

National Center for Health Statistics (2003) 'Prevalence of Overweight Among Children and Adolescents: United States, 1999–2000', www.cdc.gov/nghs/products/pubs/pubd/hestats/overwght99.htm, Hyattsville MD: National Center for Health Statistics, accessed 22 December 2003.

Oakley, A. (1984) *The Captured Womb: A History of Medical Care of Pregnant Women*, Oxford: Blackwell.

Ogilvie-Whyte, S. (2003) 'Building a Bicycle Ramp: An Illustrated Example of the Process of Translation in Children's Everyday Play Activities', paper presented to the Childhood and Youth Studies Network, Department of Applied Social Science, University of Stirling, Scotland, 30 April 2003.

Orbach, S. (1986) *Fat is a Feminist Issue: How to Lose Weight Permanently – Without Dieting*, London: Arrow Books.

Orellana, M.F., Thorne, B., Chee, A. and Lam, W.S.E. (1998/2001) 'Transnational Childhoods: The Deployment, Development and Participation of Children in Processes of Family Migration', Paper presented at 14th World Congress of the International Sociological Association, Montreal, July 1998. Revised to appear in *Social Problems Journal*, November 2001.

Oxley, H., Dang, T.-T., Forster, M.F. and Pellizzari, M. (2001) 'Income Inequalities and Poverty among Children and Households in Selected OECD Countries', in Vleminekx, K. and Smeeding, T.M. (eds), *Child Well-being, Child Poverty and Child Policy in Modern Nations*, Bristol: Policy Press.

Oyama, S. (1985) *The Ontogeny of Information: Developmental Systems and Evolution*, Cambridge: Cambridge University Press.

Pagel, M.D. and Harvey, P.H. (2002) 'Evolution of the Juvenile Period in Mammals', in Pereira, M.E. and Fairbanks, L.A. (eds), *Juvenile Primates: Life History, Development and Behaviour*, Chicago, IL: Chicago University Press.

Parliamentary Office of Science and Technology (2003) *Childhood Obesity*, London: Parliamentary Office of Science and Technology.

Parrenas, R.H. (2001) *Servants of Globalization: Women, Migration, and Domestic Work*, Stanford, CA: Stanford University Press

Pearson, G. (1983) *Hooligan: A History of Respectable Fears*, London: Macmillan.

Pereira, M.E. (2002) 'Juvenility in Animals', in Pereira, M.E. and Fairbanks, L.A. (eds), *Juvenile Primates: Life History, Development and Behaviour*, Chicago, IL: Chicago University Press.

Pereira, M.E. and Fairbanks, L.A. (2002) 'What are Juvenile Primates All About?', in Pereira, M.E. and Fairbanks, L.A. (eds), *Juvenile Primates: Life History, Development and Behaviour*, Chicago, IL: Chicago University Press.

Pickering, A. (ed.) (1992) *Science as Practice and Culture*, Chicago, IL: University of Chicago Press.

Place, B. (2000) 'Constructing the Bodies of Ill Children in the Intensive Care Unit', in Prout, A. (ed.), *The Body, Childhood and Society*, London: Macmillan.

Platt, A.M. (1977) *The Child Savers: The Invention of Delinquency*, Chicago, IL: Chicago University Press.

Plowman, L., Prout, A. and Sime, D. (2003) 'The Technologisation of Childhood? Report of a Pilot Study', Mimeo, Faculty of Human Sciences, University of Stirling.

Plowman, L. and Luckin, R. (2003) *Exploring and Mapping Interactivity with Digital Toy Technology: Summary of Findings*, Report to ESRC/EPSRC, February, www.ioe.stir.ac.uk/CACHET/publications.htm.

Pollock, L. (1983) *Forgotten Children: Parent–Child Relations from 1500 to 1900*, Cambridge: Cambridge University Press.

Population Reference Bureau (2003) *2003 World Population Data Sheet*, PDF download, 12 October, www.prb.org/.

Postman, N. (1983) *The Disappearance of Childhood*, London: W.H. Allen.

Prendergast, S. (1992) *This is the Time to Grow Up: Girls' Experiences of Menstruation in School*, Cambridge: Health Promotion Trust.

Prendergast, S. (2000) '"To Become Dizzy in Our Turning": Girls, Body Maps and Gender as Childhood Ends', in Prout, A. (ed.), *The Body, Childhood and Society*, London: Macmillan.

Press, N. and Browner, C.H. (1997) 'Why Women Say Yes to Prenatal Diagnosis', *Social Science and Medicine*, 45 (7): 979–89.

Pringle, K. (1998) *Children and Social Welfare in Europe*, Buckingham: Open University Press.

Prior, P. (1997) 'ADHD/Hyperkinetic Disorder – How Should Educational Psychologists and Other Practitioners Respond to the Emerging Phenomenon of School Children Diagnosed as Having ADHD?', *Emotional and Behavioural Difficulties*, 2: 15–27.

Prout, A. (2000a) 'Control and Self-Realisation in Late Modern Childhoods', Special Millenium Edition of *Children and Society*, 14 (4): 304–15.

Prout, A (2000b) 'Childhood Bodies, Construction, Agency and Hybridity', in Prout, A. (ed.), *The Body, Childhood and Society*, London: Macmillan.

Prout, A. (2003) 'Participation, Policy and the Changing Conditions of Childhood', in Hallett, C. and Prout, A. (eds), *Hearing the Voices of Children: Social Policy for a New Century*, London: Falmer Press.

Prout, A. and James, A. (1990/1997) 'A New Paradigm for the Sociology of Childhood? Provenance, Promise and Problems', in James, A. and Prout, A. (eds), *Constructing and Reconstructing Childhood: Contemporary Issues in the Sociological Study of Childhood*, Basingstoke: Falmer Press (2nd revised edn, London: Falmer Press).

Qvortrup, J. (1994) 'Introduction', in Qvortrup, J., Bardy, M. and Wintersberger, H. (eds), *Childhood Matters: Social Theory, Practice and Politics*, Aldershot: Avebury.

Qvortrup, J. (2000) 'Macroanalysis of Childhood', in Christensen, P. and James, A. (eds), *Research with Children: Perspectives and Practices*, London: Falmer.

Qvortrup, J., Bardy, M., Sgritta, G. and Wintersberger, H. (eds) (1994) *Childhood Matters: Social Theory, Practice and Politics*, Aldershot: Avebury.

Richards, M.P.M. (ed.) (1974) *The Integration of a Child into a Social World*, Cambridge: Cambridge University Press.

Richards, M.P.M. and Light, P. (1986) *Children in Social Worlds: Development in a Social Context*, Cambridge: Polity Press.

Ridge, T. (2002) *Childhood and Social Exclusion: From a Child's Perspective*, Bristol: Policy Press.

Rorty, R. (1981) *Philosophy and the Mirror of Nature*, Princeton, NJ: Princeton University Press.

Rose, N. (1989) *Governing the Soul*, London: Routledge.

Rose, S., Lewontin, R.C. and Kamin, L.J. (1984) *Not in Our Genes: Biology, Ideology and Human Nature*, Harmondsworth: Penguin.

Rothman, B.K. (1988) *The Tentative Pregnancy: Prenatal Diagnosis and the Future of Motherhood*, London: Pandora.

Rubenstein, D.I. (2002) 'On the Evolution of Juvenile Life-Styles in Mammals', in Pereira, M.E. and Fairbanks, L.A. (eds), *Juvenile Primates: Life History, Development and Behaviour*, Chicago, IL: Chicago University Press.

Rutter, J. and Candappa, M. (1998) *Why Do They Have To Fight? Refugee Children's Stories from Bosnia, Somalia, Sri Lanka and Turkey*, London: Refugee Council.

Ruxton, S. (1996) *Children in Europe*, London: National Children's Homes.

Schapin, S. and Scheffer, S. (1985) *Leviathan and the Air Pump: Hobbes, Boyle and the Experimental Life*, Princeton, NJ: Princeton University Press.

Scheper-Hughes, N. and Hoffman, D. (1988) 'Brazilian Apartheid: Street Kids and the Struggle for Urban Space', in Scheper-Hughes, N. and Sargent, C. (eds), *Small Wars: The Cultural Politics of Childhood*, Berkeley, CA: University of California Press.

Seccombe, W. (1993) *Weathering the Storm: Working Class Families from the Industrial Revolution to the Fertility Decline*, London: Verso.

Selwyn, N. (2003) ' "Doing IT for the Kids": Re-Examining Children, Computers and the "Information Society" ', *Media, Culture and Society*, 25: 351–78.

Sgritta, G. (1994) 'The Generational Division of Welfare: Equity and Conflict', in Qvortrup, J., Bardy, M., Sgritta, G. and Wintersberger, H. (eds), *Childhood Matters: Social Theory, Practice and Politics*, Aldershot: Avebury.

Shakespeare, T. (1998) 'Choices and Rights: Eugenics, Genetics and Disability Equality', *Disability and Society*, 13 (5): 655–81.

Shakespeare, T. (1999) 'Losing the Plot? Medical and Activist Discourses of Contemporary Genetics and Disability', *Sociology of Health and Illness*, 21 (5): 669–88.

Shilling, C. (1993) *The Body and Social Theory*, London: Sage.

Shinn, M. and Rapkin, B.D. (2000) 'Cross-Level Research without Cross-Ups in Community Psychology', in Rappaport, J. and Seidman, E. (eds), *Handbook of Community Psychology*, New York: Kluwer Academic/Plenum Publishers.

Shrag, P. and Divoky, D. (1975) *The Myth of the Hyperactive Child*, Pantheon: New York.

Simpson, B. (1998) *Changing Families: An Ethnographic Approach to Divorce and Separation*, Oxford: Berg.

Simpson, B. (2000) 'The Body as a Site of Contestation in School', in Prout, A. (ed.), *The Body, Childhood and Society*, London: Macmillan.

Singh, I. (2002) 'Biology in Context: Social and Cultural Perspectives on ADHD', *Children and Society*, 16: 360–7.

Sirota, R. (2001) 'Birthday, A Modern Ritual of Socialisation', in du Bois-Raymond, M., Sunker, H. and Kruger, H. (eds), *Childhood in Europe: Approaches – Trends – Findings*, New York: Peter Lang.

Sirota, R. (2002) 'When the Birthday Invitation Knocks Again on the Door: Learning and Construction of Manners', *Zeitschrift für Qualitative Bildungs-Beratung und Socialforschung*, 1.

Social Exclusion Unit (1998) *Truancy and School Exclusion Report by the Social Exclusion Unit*, London: Social Exclusion Unit.

Stainton-Rogers, R. and Stainton-Rogers, W. (1992) *Stories of Childhood: Shifting Agendas of Child Concern*, London: Harvester/Wheatsheaf.

Stanford, C. (2001) *Significant Others: The Ape–Human Continuum and the Quest for Human Nature*, New York: Basic Books.

Stanworth, M. (ed.) (1987) *Reproductive Technologies: Gender, Motherhood and Medicine*, Cambridge: Polity Press.

Steadman, C. (1982) *The Tidy House*, London: Virago.

Steinberg, S. and Kincheloe, J. (1997) (eds) *Kinderculture: The Corporate Construction of Childhood*, Boulder, CO: Westview.

Strathern, M. (1991) *Partial Connections*, Savage, MD: Rowman & Littlefield.

Strathern, M. (1992) *After Nature: English Kinship in the Late Twentieth Century*, Cambridge: Cambridge University Press.

Susser, M.W. and Watson, W. (1962) *Sociology in Medicine*, Oxford: Oxford University Press.

Szasz, T. (1961) *The Myth of Mental Illness*, New York: Free Press.

Thompson, D. (1989) 'The Welfare State and Generational Conflict: Winners and Losers', in Johnson, P., Conrad, C. and Thompson, D. (eds), *Workers versus Pensioners: Intergenerational Justice in an Ageing World*, Manchester: Manchester University Press.

Thorne, B. (1987) 'Re-visioning Women and Social Change: Where are the Children?', *Gender and Society*, 1: 85–109.

Thorne, B. (1993) *Gender Play: Boys and Girls in School*, New Brunswick, NJ: Rutgers University Press.

Thorne, B. (2000) 'Children's Agency and Theories of Care', Paper to the Final Conference of the ESRC Children 5–16 Research Programme, London, 21 October.

Thorne, B. (2004, forthcoming) 'Unpacking School Lunchtime: Structure, Practice and the Negotiation of Difference', Paper to the Conference of the MacArthur Network on Successful Pathways through Middle Childhood. To be published in Cooper, R., García Coll, C., Bartko. T., Davis, H. and Chatman, C. (eds), *Hills of Gold: Rethinking Diversity and Contexts as Resources for Children's Developmental Pathways*, Mahow, NJ: Lawrence Erlbaum.

Treichler, P. (1990) 'Feminism, Medicine and the Meaning of Childbirth', in Jacobus, M., Keller, E.F. and Shuttleworth, S. (eds), *Body/Politics: Women and the Discourses of Science*, London: Routledge.

Turkle, S. (1997) *Life on the Screen: Identity in the Age of the Internet*, London: Phoenix.

Turkle, S. (1998) 'Cyborg Babies and Cy-Dough Plasm: Ideas about Self and Life in the Culture of Simulation', in Davis-Floyd, R. and Dumit, J. (eds), *Cyborg Babies: From Techno-Sex to Techno-Tots*, London: Routledge.

Turner, B.S. (1984) *The Body and Society: Explorations in Social Theory*, Oxford: Blackwell.

Turner, B.S. (1992) *Regulating Bodies: Essays in Medical Sociology*, London: Routledge.

Turner, T. (1994) 'Bodies and Anti-Bodies: Flesh and Fetish in Contemporary Social Theory', in Csordas, T.J. (ed.), *Embodiment and Experience: The Existential Ground of Culture and Self*, Cambridge: Cambridge University Press.

UNICEF (1996) *The State of the World's Children*, Oxford: Oxford University Press for UNICEF.

UNICEF (2001) *We the Children*, New York: UNICEF

University of Texas (2003) 'The Passing of Ilya Priogine', web page at order.ph.utexas.edu/people/Prigogine.htm, accessed January 2004.

Urry, J. (2000) *Sociology Beyond Societies: Mobilities for the Twenty-First Century*, London: Routledge.

US Department of Health and Human Resources (1998) *Trends in the Well-Being of America's Children and Youth*, Washington: US Department of Health and Human Resources.

Valentine, G. and Holloway, S.L. (2002) 'Cyberkids? Children's Identities and Social Networks in On-Line and Off-Line Worlds', *Annals of the Association of American Geographers*, 92 (2): 302–19.

Vattimo, G. (1992) *The Transparent Society*, Cambridge: Polity Press.

Vygotsky, L.S. (1962) *Thought and Language*, Cambridge, MA: MIT Press.

Vygotsky, L.S. (1978) *Mind in Society*, Cambridge, MA: Harvard University Press.

Wajcman, J. (1991) *Feminism Confronts Technology*, Pennsylvania: Pennsylvania University Press.

Warner, R.R. (1984) 'Delayed Reproduction as a Response to Sexual Selection in a Coral Reef Fish: A Test of Life Historical Consequences', *Evolution*, 38: 148–62.

Wellcome Trust (1998) *Public Perspectives on Human Cloning*, London: Wellcome Trust.

Wilkinson, R. (2000) *Mind the Gap: Hierarchies, Health and Human Evolution (Darwinism Today)*, London: Weidenfeld & Nicholson.

Wilson, E.O. (1980) *Sociobiology*, Cambridge, MA: Belknap Press of Harvard University Press.

Winn, M. (1984) *Children without Childhood*, Harmondsworth: Penguin.

Woodhead, M. (1999) 'Reconstructing Developmental Psychology, Some First Steps', *Children and Society*, 13 (1): 3–19.

Woodhead, M. (2003) 'Childhood Studies: Past, Present and Future', Keynote lecture at Open University Conference, June.

Zeiher, H. (2001) 'Children's Islands in Space and Time: The Impact of Spatial Differentiation on Children's Ways of Shaping Social Life', in du Bois-Reymond, M., Sunker, H. and Kruger, H.-H. (eds), *Childhood in Europe: Approaches – Trends – Findings*, New York: Peter Lang.

Zeiher, H. (2002) 'Shaping Daily Life in Urban Environments', in Christensen, P. and O'Brien, M. (eds), *Children in the City: Home, Neighbourhood and Community*, London: Falmer Press.

Index